EVIDENCE-BASED TREATMENT PLANNING FOR SUBSTANCE USE DISORDERS

EVIDENCE–BASED TREATMENT PLANNING FOR SUBSTANCE USE DISORDERS

DVD COMPANION WORKBOOK

ARTHUR E. JONGSMA, JR.
AND
TIMOTHY J. BRUCE

WILEY

John Wiley & Sons, Inc.

Contents

Introduction   vii

Chapter 1 What Are Substance Use Disorders?   1

Chapter 2 What Are the Six Steps in Building a Treatment Plan?   5

Chapter 3 What Is the Brief History of the Empirically
           Supported Treatments Movement?   7

Chapter 4 What Are the Identified Empirically Supported
           Treatments for Substance Use Disorders?   13

Chapter 5 How Do You Integrate Empirically Supported
           Treatments Into Treatment Planning?   34

Closing Remarks and Resources   57

Appendix A A Sample Evidence-Based Treatment Plan
            for Substance Use Disorders   59

Appendix B Chapter Review Test Questions
            and Answers Explained   62

Introduction

This *Workbook* is a companion to the *Evidence-Based Treatment Planning for Substance Use Disorders DVD*, which is focused on informing mental health therapists, addiction counselors, and students in these fields about evidence-based psychological treatment planning.

Organization

In this *Workbook* you will find in each chapter:

- Summary highlights of content shown in the DVD
- Chapter review discussion questions
- Chapter review test questions
- Chapter references
- Key points for review

In appropriate chapters, the references are divided into those for *empirical support*, those for *clinical resources*, and those for *bibliotherapy resources*. Empirical support references are selected studies or reviews of the empirical work supporting the efficacy of the empirically supported treatments (ESTs) discussed in the chapter. The clinical resources are books, manuals, or other resources for clinicians that describe the application, or "how to," of the treatments discussed. The bibliotherapy resources are selected publications and Web sites relevant to the DVD content that may be helpful to clinicians, clients, or laypersons.

Examples of client homework are included at www.wiley.com/go/sudwb They are designed to enhance understanding of therapeutic interventions, in addition to being potentially useful clinically.

Appendix A contains an example of an evidence-based treatment plan for Substance Use Disorders. In Appendix B, correct and incorrect answers to all chapter review test questions are explained.

Chapter Points

This DVD is electronically marked with chapter points that delineate the beginning of discussion sections throughout the program. You may skip to any one of these chapter points on the DVD by clicking on the forward arrow. The chapter points for this program are as follows:

- ➤ Defining Substance Use Disorders
- ➤ Six Steps in Building a Psychotherapy Treatment Plan
- ➤ Brief History of the EST Movement
- ➤ ESTs for Substance Use Disorders
- ➤ Integrating ESTs for Substance Use Disorders Into a Treatment Plan
- ➤ An Evidence-Based Treatment Plan for Substance Use Disorders

Series Rationale

Evidence-based practice (EBP) is steadily becoming the standard of mental health care as it has in medical health care. Borrowing from the Institute of Medicine's definition (Institute of Medicine, 2001), the American Psychological Association (APA) has defined EBP as "the integration of the best available research with clinical expertise in the context of patient characteristics, culture, and preferences" (American Psychological Association Presidential Task Force on Evidence-Based Practice (APA), 2006).

Professional organizations such as the American Psychological Association, the National Association of Social Workers, and the American Psychiatric Association, as well as consumer organizations such the National Alliance for the Mentally Ill (NAMI), are endorsing EBP. At the federal level, a major joint initiative of the National Institute of Mental Health and Department of Health and Human Services' Substance Abuse and Mental Health Services Administration (SAMHSA) focuses on promoting, implementing, and evaluating evidence-based mental health programs and practices within state mental health systems (APA, 2006). In some practice settings, EBP is even becoming mandated. It is clear that the call for evidence-based practice is being increasingly sounded.

Unfortunately, many mental health care providers cannot or do not stay abreast of results from clinical research and how they can inform their practices. Although it has rightfully been argued that the relevance of some research to the clinician's needs is weak, there are products of clinical research whose efficacy has been well established and whose effectiveness in the community setting has received support. Clinicians and clinicians-in-training interested in empirically informing their treatments could benefit from educational programs that make this goal more easily attainable.

This series of DVDs and companion workbooks is designed to introduce clinicians and students to the process of empirically informing their psychotherapy treatment plans. The series begins with an introduction to the efforts to identify research-supported treatments and how the products of these efforts can be used to inform treatment planning. The other programs in the series focus on empirically informed treatment planning for each of several commonly seen clinical problems. In each problem-focused DVD, issues involved in defining or diagnosing the presenting problem are reviewed. Research-supported treatments for the problem are described, as well as the process used to identify them. Viewers are then systematically guided through the process of creating a treatment plan, and shown how the plan can be informed by goals, objectives, and interventions consistent with those of the identified research-supported treatments. Example vignettes of selected interventions are also provided.

This series is intended to be educational and informative in nature and not meant to be a substitute for clinical training in the specific interventions discussed and demonstrated. References to empirical support of the treatments described, clinical resource material, and training opportunities are provided.

Presenters

Dr. Art Jongsma is the Series Editor and co-author of the Practice*Planners*® series published by John Wiley & Sons. He has authored or co-authored more than 40 books in this series. Among the books included in this series are the highly regarded *The Complete Adult Psychotherapy Treatment Planner*, *The Adolescent* and *The Child Psychotherapy Treatment Planners*, and *The Addiction Treatment Planner*. All of these books, along with *The Severe and Persistent Mental Illness Treatment Planner*, *The Family Therapy Treatment Planner*, *The Couples Psychotherapy Treatment Planner*,

Exhibit I.1   Dr. Tim Bruce and Dr. Art Jongsma

The Older Adult Psychotherapy Treatment Planner, and *The Veterans and Active Duty Military Psychotherapy Treatment Planner*, are informed with objectives and interventions that are supported by research evidence.

Dr. Jongsma also created the clinical record management software tool Thera*Scribe*®, which uses point-and-click technology to easily develop, store, and print treatment plans, progress notes, and homework assignments. He has conducted treatment planning and software training workshops for mental health professionals around the world.

Dr. Jongsma's clinical career began as a psychologist in a large private psychiatric hospital. He worked in the hospital for about 10 years and then transitioned to outpatient work in his own private practice clinic, Psychological Consultants, in Grand Rapids, Michigan, for 25 years. He has been writing best-selling books and software for mental health professionals since 1995. He lives in a suburb of Grand Rapids with his wife, Judy.

Dr. Timothy Bruce is a Professor and Associate Chair of the Department of Psychiatry and Behavioral Medicine at the University of Illinois, College of Medicine in Peoria, Illinois, where he also directs medical student education. He is a licensed clinical psychologist who completed his graduate training at SUNY-Albany under the mentorship of Dr. David Barlow and his residency training at Wilford Hall Medical Center under the direction of Dr. Robert Klepac. In addition to maintaining an active clinical practice at the university, Dr. Bruce has written numerous publications, including books, professional journal articles, book chapters, and professional educational materials, many on the topic of evidence-based practice. Most recently, he has served as the developmental editor empirically informing Dr. Jongsma's best-selling Practice*Planners*® series.

Dr. Bruce is also Executive Director of the Center for the Dissemination of Evidence-Based Mental Health Practices, a state- and federally funded initiative to disseminate evidence-based psychological and pharmacological practices across Illinois. Highly recognized as an educator, Dr. Bruce has received nearly two dozen awards for his teaching of students and professionals during his career.

References

American Psychological Association Presidential Task Force on Evidence-Based Practice. (2006). Evidence-based practice in psychology. *American Psychologist*, *61*, 271–285.

Berghuis, D., Jongsma, A., & Bruce, T. (2006). *The severe and persistent mental illness treatment planner* (2nd ed.). Hoboken, NJ: Wiley.

Dattilio, F., Jongsma, A., & Davis, S. (2009). *The family therapy treatment planner* (2nd ed.). Hoboken, NJ: Wiley.

Institute of Medicine. (2001). *Crossing the quality chasm: A new health system for the 21st century*. Washington, DC: National Academy Press.

Jongsma, A., Peterson, M., & Bruce, T. (2006). *The complete adult psychotherapy treatment planner* (4th ed.). Hoboken, NJ: Wiley.

Jongsma, A., Peterson, M., McInnis, W., & Bruce, T. (2006a). *The adolescent psychotherapy treatment planner* (4th ed.). Hoboken, NJ: Wiley.

Jongsma, A., Peterson, M., McInnis, W., & Bruce, T. (2006b). *The child psychotherapy treatment planner* (4th ed.). Hoboken, NJ: Wiley.

Moore, B., & Jongsma, A. (2009). *The veterans and active duty military psychotherapy treatment planner*. Hoboken, NJ: Wiley.

Perkinson, R., Jongsma, A., & Bruce, T. (2009). *The addiction treatment planner* (4th ed.). Hoboken, NJ: Wiley.

CHAPTER 1

What Are Substance Use Disorders?

Defining Substance Use Disorders

In this program, we are going to discuss evidence-based treatment planning for substance use disorders (SUD). Let's begin by looking at the criteria for the disorder according to the *Diagnostic and Statistical Manual of Mental Disorders* (DSM). The *DSM* distinguishes the more debilitating condition of Substance Dependence from Substance Abuse. The criteria for Substance Dependence are summarized in Figure 1.1.

Figure 1.1

DSM Criteria for Substance Dependence

Diagnostically, substance *dependence* is defined by a maladaptive pattern of alcohol or drug use that leads to significant impairment or distress, as manifested by three (or more) of the following, occurring at any time in the same 12-month period:

(1) Tolerance, as defined by either of the following:

    (a)   a need for markedly increased amounts of the substance to achieve intoxication or desired effect

    (b)   markedly diminished effect with continued use of the same amount of the substance

(2) Withdrawal, as manifested by either of the following:

    (a)   2 or more of the following, developing within several hours to a few days of reduction in heavy or prolonged alcohol or substance use:

- Sweating or rapid pulse
- Increased hand tremor
- Insomnia
- Nausea or vomiting
- Physical agitation
- Anxiety
- Transient visual, tactile, or auditory hallucinations or illusions
- Grand mal seizures

(continued)

(b)   The same (or a closely related) substance is taken to relieve or avoid withdrawal symptoms

(3) The substance is often taken in larger amounts or over a longer period than was intended.

(4) There is a persistent desire or unsuccessful efforts to cut down or control substance use.

(5) A great deal of time is spent in activities necessary to obtain the substance (e.g., visiting multiple doctors or driving long distances), use the substance (e.g., drink all night), or recover from its effects.

(6) Important social, occupational, or recreational activities are given up or reduced because of substance use.

(7) The substance use is continued despite knowledge of having a persistent or recurrent physical or psychological problem that is likely to have been caused or exacerbated by the substance (e.g., current cocaine use despite recognition of cocaine-induced depression, or continued drinking despite recognition that an ulcer was made worse by alcohol consumption).

From the *Diagnostic and Statistical Manual of Mental Disorders-IV-TR* (APA, 2000)

Figure 1.2

DSM Specifiers for Substance Dependence

SPECIFY IF:

• With Physiological Dependence: Evidence of tolerance or withdrawal
• Without Physiological Dependence: No evidence of tolerance or withdrawal

COURSE SPECIFIERS:

• Early Full Remission
• Early Partial Remission
• Sustained Full Remission
• Sustained Partial Remission
• On Agonist Therapy
• In a Controlled Environment

From the *Diagnostic and Statistical Manual of Mental Disorders-IV-TR* (APA, 2000)

The *DSM-IV* requires the diagnostician to specify whether physiological dependence is present or absent as indicated by tolerance or withdrawal in the client. Therefore, the specifier "With Physiological Dependence" or "Without Physiological Dependence" must be selected.

Lastly, there are also six "course specifiers." The four remission specifiers can be applied only after none of the criteria for Abuse or Dependence has been present for at least one month. The other two specifiers apply if the individual is on agonist medication therapy such as methadone or the individual is in a controlled environment (Figure 1.2).

Criteria for Substance Abuse

The essential feature of substance *abuse* is a maladaptive pattern of substance use evidenced by recurrent and significant adverse consequences related to the repeated use. Diagnostically, the pattern of alcohol or drug use must result in significant impairment or distress, as manifested by one (or more) of the following, occurring within a 12-month period:

1. Because of intoxication or other substance-related symptoms, the person fails to fulfill major role obligations at work, home, or school. For example, there may be repeated absences or poor work performance; suspensions or expulsions from school; or neglect of children or household responsibilities.
2. There may be recurrent substance use when it is physically hazardous, such as while driving an automobile or operating a machine.
3. There may be recurrent substance-related legal problems such as arrests for substance-related disorderly conduct.
4. There may be continued substance use despite persistent social or interpersonal problems such as arguments with family or friends about consequences of intoxication or physical fights.

Unlike the criteria for substance dependence, the criteria for substance abuse do not include tolerance, withdrawal, or a pattern of compulsive use. Instead, they include only the harmful consequences of repeated use (Figure 1.3).

Figure 1.3

DSM Criteria for Substance Abuse

A. A maladaptive pattern of substance use leading to clinically significant impairment or distress, as manifested by one (or more) of the following, occurring within a 12-month period:

(1) Recurrent substance use resulting in a failure to fulfill major role obligations at work, school, or home

(2) Recurrent substance use in situations in which it is physically hazardous

(3) Recurrent substance-related legal problems

(4) Continued substance use despite having persistent or recurrent social or interpersonal problems caused or exacerbated by the effects of the substance

B. The symptoms have never met the criteria for Substance Dependence for this class of substance.

From the *Diagnostic and Statistical Manual of Mental Disorders-IV-TR* (APA, 2000)

Key Points

SUBSTANCE DEPENDENCE VERSUS SUBSTANCE ABUSE

- *Substance dependence* is defined by a maladaptive pattern of alcohol or drug use that leads to significant impairment or distress.
- It is manifested by three (or more) criteria indicative of physiological tolerance, withdrawal, or chronic use.
- The diagnosis of dependence may or may not include physiological dependence.
- *Substance abuse* is a maladaptive pattern of substance use leading to clinically significant impairment or distress and manifested by recurrent and significant adverse consequences related to the repeated use of substances.
- Unlike the criteria for substance dependence, the criteria for substance abuse do *not* include a possibility of tolerance, withdrawal, or a pattern of compulsive use. Instead, they include only the harmful consequences of repeated use.

Chapter Review

1. What are the seven diagnostic criteria for substance dependence, three (or more) of which must be evident within the same 12-month period?
2. What are the four diagnostic criteria for substance abuse, one (or more) of which must be evident within the same 12-month period?

Chapter Review Test Questions

1. After several months of substance use, Bill has begun using the substance when he awakens in the morning with some shakes and feelings of anxiety. He states that, "It calms me." Diagnostically, this pattern of use is considered a manifestation of which of the following:

   A. Anxiety
   B. Insomnia
   C. Tolerance
   D. Withdrawal

2. True or False: According to the *DSM*, substance dependence is not diagnosed unless there is evidence of physiological tolerance or withdrawal.

Reference

American Psychiatric Association. (2000). *Diagnostic and statistical manual of mental disorders* (4th ed., text rev.; DSM-IV-TR). Washington, DC: American Psychiatric Association.

CHAPTER 2

What Are the Six Steps in Building a Treatment Plan?

Step 1: Identify primary and secondary problems
- ➤ Use evidence-based psychosocial assessment procedures to determine the most significant problem or problems related to current distress, disability, or both.

Step 2: Describe the problem's behavioral manifestations (symptom pattern)
- ➤ Note how the problem(s) is evident in your particular client. These features may correspond to the diagnostic criteria for the problem.

Step 3: Make a diagnosis based on *DSM/ICD* criteria
- ➤ Based on an evaluation of the client's complete clinical presentation, determine the appropriate diagnosis using the process and criteria described in the *DSM* or the *ICD*.

Step 4: Specify long-term goals
- ➤ These goal statements need not be crafted in measurable terms, but are broader and indicate a desired general positive outcome of treatment.

Step 5: Create short-term objectives
- ➤ Objectives for the client to achieve should be stated in measurable or observable terms so accountability is enhanced.

Step 6: Select therapeutic interventions
- ➤ Interventions are the actions of the clinician within the therapeutic alliance designed to help the client accomplish the treatment objectives. There should be at least one intervention planned for each client objective.

Key Point

One important aspect of effective treatment planning is that each plan should be tailored to the individual client's particular problems and needs. Treatment plans should not be boilerplate, even if clients have similar problems. Consistent with the definition of an evidence-based practice, the individual's strengths and weaknesses, unique stressors, cultural and social network, family circumstances, and symptom patterns must be considered in developing a treatment strategy. Clinicians should rely on their own good clinical judgment and plan a treatment that is appropriate for the distinctive individual with whom they are working.

Chapter Review

1. What are the six steps involved in developing a psychotherapy treatment plan?

Chapter Review Test Questions

1. Some patients with a substance use disorder demonstrate physiological tolerance; some do not. Some show problems in one area of functioning, whereas others may not. In which step of treatment planning would you record the particular expressions of substance use disorder for your individual client?

   A. Creating short-term objectives
   B. Describing the problem's manifestations
   C. Identifying the primary problem
   D. Selecting treatment interventions

2. The statement "Learn and implement strategies for identifying, preventing, or coping with high-risk situations for relapse back into substance use" is an example of which of the following steps in psychotherapy treatment planning?

   A. A primary problem
   B. A short-term objective
   C. A symptom manifestation
   D. A treatment intervention

Chapter References

American Psychological Association Presidential Task Force on Evidence-Based Practice. (2006). Evidence-based practice in psychology. *American Psychologist, 61*, 271–185.

Jongsma, A. (2005). Psychotherapy treatment plan writing. In G. P. Koocher, J. C. Norcross, & S. S. Hill (Eds.), *Psychologists' desk reference* (2nd ed., pp. 232–236). New York, NY: Oxford University Press.

Jongsma, A., Peterson, M., & Bruce, T. (2006). *The complete adult psychotherapy treatment planner* (4th ed.). Hoboken, NJ: Wiley.

Jongsma, A., Peterson, M., McInnis, W., & Bruce, T. (2006). *The adolescent psychotherapy treatment planner* (4th ed.). Hoboken, NJ: Wiley.

CHAPTER 3

What Is the Brief History of the Empirically Supported Treatments Movement?

In the United States, the effort to identify empirically supported treatments (EST) began with an initiative of the American Psychological Association's Division 12, The Society of Clinical Psychology.

In 1993, APA's Division 12 President David Barlow initiated a task group, chaired by Diane Chambless. The group was charged to review the psychotherapy outcome literature to identify psychological treatments whose efficacy had been demonstrated through clinical research. This group was originally called the Task Force on the Promotion and Dissemination of Psychological Procedures, and was later reorganized under the Task Force on Psychological Interventions.

Process Used to Identify ESTs

Reviewers established two primary sets of criteria for judging the evidence base supporting any particular therapy. One was labeled *well-established*, the other *probably efficacious* (Fig. 3.1).

Key Point

Division 12's criteria for a well-established treatment are similar to the standards used by the United States Food and Drug Administration (FDA) to evaluate the safety and efficacy of proposed medications. The FDA requires demonstration that a proposed medication is significantly superior to a nonspecific control treatment (a pill placebo) in at least two randomized controlled trials conducted by independent research groups. Division 12's criteria for a well-established treatment require the equivalent of this standard as well as other features relevant to judging a psychological treatment's efficacy (e.g., a clear description of the treatment and study participants). By extension, if the FDA were to evaluate psychotherapies using the criteria they use for medication, it would allow sale of those judged to be well-established.

Figure 3.1

Specific Criteria for Well-Established and Probably Efficacious Treatments

Criteria for a Well-Established Treatment

For a psychological treatment to be considered *well-established*, the evidence base supporting it had to be characterized by the following:

  I. At least two good between-group design experiments demonstrating efficacy in one or more of the following ways:

  A. Superior (statistically significantly so) to pill or psychological placebo or to another treatment

  B. Equivalent to an already established treatment in experiments with adequate sample sizes

OR

  II. A large series of single-case design experiments (n > 9) demonstrating efficacy. These experiments must have:

  A. Used good experimental designs

  B. Compared the intervention to another treatment as in IA

Further Criteria for Both I and II:
III. Experiments must be conducted with treatment manuals.

IV. Characteristics of the client samples must be clearly specified.

  V. Effects must have been demonstrated by at least two different investigators or investigating teams.

Criteria for a Probably Efficacious Treatment

For a psychological treatment to be considered *probably efficacious*, the evidence base supporting it had to meet the following criteria:

  I. Two experiments showing the treatment is superior (statistically significantly so) to a waiting-list control group.

OR

  II. One or more experiments meeting the Well-Established Treatment Criteria IA or IB, III, and IV, but not V.

OR

  III. A small series of single-case design experiments (n > 3) otherwise meeting Well-Established Treatment

---

Adapted from "Update on Empirically Validated Therapies, II," by D. L. Chambless, M. J. Baker, D. H. Baucom, L. E. Beutler, K. S. Calhoun, P. Crits-Christoph, . . . & S. R. Woody, 1998, *The Clinical Psychologist*, 51(1), 3–16.

Products of EST Reviews

The products of these reviews can be found in the Division 12 groups' final two reports.

> ➤ In the first report, 47 ESTs are identified (Chambless et al., 1996).
> ➤ In the final report, the list had grown to 71 ESTs (Chambless et al., 1998).
> ➤ In 1999, The Society of Clinical Psychology, Division 12, took full ownership of maintaining the growing list. The current list and information center can be found on its Web site at www.psychologicaltreatments.org

Around this same time, other groups emerged, using the same or similar criteria, to review literatures related to other populations, problems, and interventions. Examples include the following:

> ➤ Children (Lonigan & Elbert, 1998)
> ➤ Pediatric Psychology (Spirito, 1999)
> ➤ Older Adults (Gatz, 1998)
> ➤ Adult, Child, Couples, Family Therapy (Kendall & Chambless, 1998)
> ➤ Psychopharmacology and Psychological Treatments (Nathan & Gorman, 1998, 2002, 2007)
> ➤ Substance Use Disorders (Glasner-Edwards & Rawson, 2010)

For those interested in comparing and contrasting the criteria used by various review groups, see Chambless and Ollendick (2001).

TherapyAdvisor

Descriptions of the treatments identified through many of these early reviews, as well as references to the empirical work supporting them, clinical resources, and training opportunities can be found at www.therapyadvisor.com. This resource was developed by Personal Improvement Computer Systems (PICS) with funding from the National Institute of Mental Health and in consultation with members of the original Division 12 task groups. Information found on TherapyAdvisor is provided by the primary author/researcher(s) of the given EST.

Selected Organizational Reviewers of Evidence–Based Psychological Treatments and Practices

> ➤ Great Britain is at the forefront of the effort to identify evidence-based treatments and develop guidelines for practice. The latest products of their work can be found at the Web site for the National Institute for Health and Clinical Excellence (NICE): http://www.nice.org.uk/

➤ The Substance Abuse and Mental Health Services Administration (SAMHSA) has an initiative to evaluate, identify, and provide information on various mental health practices. Their work, entitled "The National Registry of Evidence-based Programs and Practices or NREPP," can be found online at http://www.nrepp.samhsa.gov/

➤ The Agency for Health Care Policy and Research, now called the Agency for Healthcare Research and Quality (AHRQ), has established guidelines and criteria for identifying evidence-based practices and provides links to evidence-based clinical practice guidelines for various medical and mental health problems at http://www.ahrq.gov/clinic/epcix.htm

➤ The Cochrane Collaboration is an international network of professionals who conduct systematic reviews of research in human health care and health policy. Among their products are critical reviews of psychological treatment interventions and specific intervention questions. They can be found on the Web at www.cochrane.org

➤ Currently, the American Psychological Association, Divisions 12 and 50 (The Society of Addiction Psychology), are collaborating on identifying research-supported treatments for addictions. Division 50 has a Web site with information and links to various evidence-based resources for the treatment of addictions: http://www.apa.org/divisions/div50/ebp_overview.html

➤ The National Institute on Drug Abuse (NIDA) has published evidence-based guidelines entitled *Principles of Drug Addiction Treatment: A Research-Based Guide*. This guide, as well as other resources, can be found on their Web site at http://www.nida.nih.gov/nidahome.html

➤ The National Quality Forum is a group of stakeholder organizations that has created a set of national voluntary consensus standards for a variety of conditions. Among their works are proceedings of an expert consensus workshop entitled *Evidence-Based Treatment Practices for Substance Use Disorder*, in which core treatment practices supported by scientific evidence are identified: http://www.qualityforum.org/Home.aspx

Other Reviews

Other reviews can be found in the reference section of Chapter 4 under "Empirical Support."

Chapter Review

1. How did Division 12 of the APA identify ESTs?
2. What are the primary differences between *well-established* and *probably efficacious* criteria used to identify ESTs?
3. Where can information about ESTs and evidence-based practices be found?

Chapter Review Test Questions

1. Which statement best describes the process used to identify ESTs?
   A. Consumers of mental health services nominated therapies.
   B. Experts came to a consensus based on their experiences with the treatments.
   C. Researchers submitted their works.
   D. Task groups reviewed the literature using clearly defined selection criteria for ESTs.

2. Based on the differences in their criteria, in which of the following ways are *well-established* treatments different from those classified as *probably efficacious*?
   A. Only *probably efficacious* allowed the use of single-case design experiments.
   B. Only *well-established* allowed studies comparing the treatment to a psychological placebo.
   C. Only *well-established* required demonstration by at least two different, independent investigators or investigating teams.
   D. Only *well-established* allowed studies comparing the treatment to a pill placebo.

Chapter References

Chambless, D. L., & Ollendick, T. H. (2001). Empirically supported psychological interventions: Controversies and evidence. *Annual Review of Psychology, 52,* 685–716.

Chambless, D. L., Sanderson, W. C., Shoham, V., Bennett Johnson, S., Pope, K. S., Crits-Christoph, P., . . . McCurry, S. (1996). An update on empirically validated therapies. *The Clinical Psychologist, 49,* 5–18.

Chambless, D. L., Baker, M. J., Baucom, D. H., Beutler, L. E., Calhoun, K. S., Crits-Christoph, P., . . . Woody, S. R. (1998). Update on empirically validated therapies, II. *The Clinical Psychologist, 51,* 3–16.

Gatz, M., Fiske, A., Fox, L. S., Kaskie, B., Kasl-Godley, J. E., McCallum, T., & Wetherell, J. (1998). Empirically validated psychological treatments for older adults. *Journal of Mental Health and Aging, 41,* 9–46.

Glasner-Edwards, S., & Rawson, R. (2010). Evidence-based practices in addiction treatment: Review and recommendations for public policy. *Health Policy, 97,* 93–104.

Kendall, P. C., & Chambless, D. L. (Eds.). (1998). Empirically supported psychological therapies [special issue]. *Journal of Consulting and Clinical Psychology, 66*(3), 151–162.

Lonigan, C. J., & Elbert, J. C. (Eds.). (1998). Empirically supported psychosocial interventions for children [special issue]. *Journal of Clinical Child Psychology, 27,* 138–226.

Nathan, P. E., & Gorman, J. M. (Eds.). (1998). *A guide to treatments that work.* New York, NY: Oxford University Press.

Nathan, P. E., & Gorman, J. M. (Eds.). (2002). *A guide to treatments that work* (2nd ed.). New York, NY: Oxford University Press.

Nathan, P. E., & Gorman, J. M. (Eds.). (2007). *A guide to treatments that work* (3rd ed.). New York, NY: Oxford University Press.

Spirito, A. (Ed.). (1999). Empirically supported treatments in pediatric psychology [special issue]. *Journal of Pediatric Psychology, 24,* 87–174.

4

What Are the Identified Empirically Supported Treatments for Substance Use Disorders?

Empirically informing a treatment plan as described in this series involves integrating those aspects of empirically supported treatments (ESTs) into each step of the treatment planning process discussed previously. Let's briefly look at efforts to develop and identify ESTs and evidence-based treatment guidelines for SUD.

As noted earlier, several efforts have been made to identify research-supported treatments for substance use disorders as well as to craft evidence-based practice guidelines. Examples include Finney, Wilbourne, and Moos in Nathan and Gorman's *A Guide to Treatments That Work*, the efforts of the APA's Division 12 (The Society of Clinical Psychology) and Division 50 (The Society of Addiction Psychology), the National Institute on Drug Abuse (NIDA), the National Registry of Evidence-Based Programs and Practices (NREPP), the National Institute of Clinical Excellence (NICE) in Great Britain, and the National Quality Forum. Conclusions across these various reviewers are nearly uniform in regard to which treatments they have identified as research supported and which are recommended in evidence-based practice guidelines. Let's look at these reviews and their conclusions.

The National Institute on Drug Abuse (NIDA)

In their publication, *Principles of Drug Addiction Treatment: A Research-Based Guide*, NIDA has identified several treatment approaches that have shown efficacy in the treatment of various substance use disorders. These are:

- ➤ **Cognitive-behavioral therapy** for alcohol, marijuana, cocaine, methamphetamine, and nicotine addictions
- ➤ The **community reinforcement approach** for alcohol and cocaine
- ➤ **Contingency management interventions**, also known as motivational incentives, for alcohol, stimulants, opioids, marijuana, nicotine
- ➤ **Motivational enhancement therapy** for alcohol, marijuana, nicotine

➤ The **Matrix Model** for stimulants

➤ **12-Step facilitation therapy** for alcohol, stimulants, opiates

➤ **Behavioral couples therapy** for alcoholic men and their spouses, as well as drug-abusing men and women and their significant others

Figure 4.1 provides a synopsis of conclusions drawn from the NIDA reviews.

Figure 4.1

Conclusions from the National Institute on Drug Abuse

EVIDENCE-BASED TREATMENTS FOR SUD:

- Cognitive-behavioral therapy
- The community reinforcement approach
- Contingency management interventions
- Motivational enhancement therapy
- The Matrix Model
- 12-step facilitation therapy
- Behavioral couples therapy

From NIDA, "Principles of Drug Addiction Treatment: A Research-Based Guide," available online at www.nida.nih.gov/nidahome

---

National Quality Forum

In a different, expert consensus approach, the National Quality Forum held a workshop of experts in this area and asked them to identify evidence-based practices. The proceedings of this meeting were published in a work entitled *Evidence-Based Treatment Practices for Substance Use Disorder*. In it, the expert participants identify the exact same treatments that NIDA does, but also add that family and multisystem interventions, such as multisystemic therapy, brief strategic family therapy, and multidimensional family therapy, have demonstrated efficacy for more complex substance-using, conduct-disordered adolescents.

Figure 4.2 provides a synopsis of conclusions drawn from the National Quality Forum Workshop.

Finney, Wilbourne, and Moos

In the latest edition of Nathan and Gorman's *A Guide to Treatments That Work*, Finney, Wilbourne, and Moos (2007) review the substance use disorder literature. They too cite the same list of treatments as the previous reviewers, noting that they are supported by large numbers of qualifying clinical trials—what Nathan and

Gorman refer to as Type I and II trials. They also noted therapist factors associated with better outcomes, including having interpersonal skill, empathy, and being less confrontational—factors that may lead to better therapeutic alliances with patients.

Figure 4.3 provides a synopsis of conclusions from Finney, Wilbourne, and Moos.

Figure 4.2

Conclusions from the National Quality Forum Workshop

EVIDENCE-BASED TREATMENTS FOR SUD:

- Cognitive-behavioral therapies
- Community reinforcement
- Contingency management interventions
- Motivational enhancement therapy
- The Matrix Model
- 12-Step facilitation therapy
- Behavioral couples therapy
- Family and multisystem interventions

From the National Quality Forum, *Evidence-Based Treatment Practices for Substance Use Disorder.*

Figure 4.3

Conclusions from Finney, Wilbourne, and Moos

RESEARCH-SUPPORTED TREATMENTS FOR SUD:

- Cognitive-behavioral treatments
- Community reinforcement
- Contingency management approaches
- 12-step facilitation therapy
- Behavioral couples therapy
- Family therapy interventions
- Motivational enhancement interventions

RESEARCH-SUPPORTED THERAPIST AND THERAPEUTIC RELATIONSHIP FACTORS IN THE TREATMENT OF SUD:

- Interpersonally skilled
- Empathic
- Less confrontational
- Good therapeutic alliance associated with better outcomes

From Finney, J. W., Wilbourne, P. L., & Moos, R. H. (2007). In P. E. Nathan & J. M. Gorman (eds.), *A Guide to Treatments That Work* (pp. 179–202). New York, NY: Oxford University Press.

Glasner–Edwards and Rawson: Public Policy Recommendations

Glasner-Edwards and Rawson (2010) evaluated this literature with the intent of identifying public policy recommendations and grouped treatments in terms of four recommended therapeutic skill sets. Within those categories are all of the previously identified treatments, with the notable exception of 12-step facilitation treatment, which the authors acknowledge as empirically supported. As examples of treatments that fall within each of these skill sets, the authors cited the following:

Under Use of Contingency Management Principles, they cited:

➤ Contingency management (or CM)
➤ Prize incentives
➤ Community reinforcement (with and without vouchers)

Under Motivational Interviewing Techniques, they cited:

➤ Motivational enhancement therapy
➤ Motivational interviewing
➤ Brief intervention

Under Cognitive Behavioral Coping Skills/Relapse Prevention Strategies, they cited:

➤ Cognitive-behavioral coping skills therapy
➤ Relapse prevention therapy
➤ The Matrix Model

And under Couples/Family Counseling Techniques, they cited:

➤ Behavioral couples therapy
➤ Multidimensional family therapy

These authors also identified what they labeled as "discredited treatments." They described two categories of discredited treatments based on the level of evidence supporting the designation: *certainly discredited* and *probably discredited*.

Examples of treatments they cite as certainly discredited include:

➤ Past-life therapy
➤ Neuro-linguistic programming
➤ Scared Straight

Probably discredited approaches include:

➤ DARE prevention programs
➤ Synanon-style boot camps
➤ Various medication approaches that have failed to show efficacy

Figure 4.4

Glasner-Edwards and Rawson's Public Policy Recommendations: Recommended Therapeutic Skill Sets

USE OF CONTINGENCY MANAGEMENT PRINCIPLES:

- Contingency management (CM)
- Prize incentives
- Community reinforcement (with and without vouchers)

MOTIVATIONAL INTERVIEWING TECHNIQUES:

- Motivational enhancement therapy
- Motivational interviewing
- Brief intervention

COGNITIVE-BEHAVIORAL COPING SKILLS/RELAPSE PREVENTION STRATEGIES:

- Cognitive-behavioral coping skills therapy
- Relapse prevention therapy
- The Matrix Model

COUPLES/FAMILY COUNSELING TECHNIQUES:

- Behavioral couples therapy
- Multidimensional family therapy

From Glasner-Edwards, S., & Rawson, R. (2010). Evidence-based practices in addiction treatment: Review and recommendations for public policy. *Health Policy, 97,* 93–104.

Figure 4.4 provides a synopsis of Glasner-Edwards and Rawson's public policy recommendations.

A Review of Research-Supported Treatments for Substance Use Disorders

These various reviewers are clearly uniform regarding what types of approaches are deemed to be research-supported. Let's take a brief look at the major features of each as described by NIDA.

Cognitive-Behavioral Therapy (CBT)

CBT was originally developed to prevent relapse of problem drinking, and was later adapted to treating cocaine addiction. Cognitive-behavioral strategies target learning processes that are presumed to play a critical role in the development of maladaptive behavioral patterns. Individuals learn to identify and correct problematic

---

Figure 4.5

CBT Approach to Treating SUD

CBT Focus: Identify and correct problematic thoughts and behaviors via:

- Exploring consequences of use
- Self-monitoring cravings and high-risk situations
- Developing coping strategies for risky situations
- Developing relapse prevention strategies

From NIDA, *Principles of Drug Addiction Treatment: A Research-Based Guide.*

---

thoughts and behaviors by applying a range of different skills intended to enhance self-control:

> Specific techniques include exploring the positive and negative consequences of continued use.
> Self-monitoring is used to recognize substance cravings early on and to identify high-risk situations for use.
> Strategies are developed for coping with and avoiding high-risk situations that increase the desire to use.
> A central element of this treatment is anticipating likely problems and helping patients develop effective relapse prevention strategies for managing them successfully.

Figure 4.5 provides a synopsis of the CBT approach to treating SUD.

Community Reinforcement Approach (CRA)

The Community Reinforcement Approach, or CRA Plus Vouchers, is an intensive 24-week outpatient therapy program for treatment of cocaine and alcohol addiction. It has two primary treatment goals:

1. To maintain abstinence long enough for patients to learn new life skills to help sustain it.
2. To reduce alcohol consumption for patients whose drinking is associated with cocaine use.

CRA Plus Vouchers is characterized by these five features:

1. Patients attend one or two individual counseling sessions per week, where they focus on improving family relations, learning a variety of skills to minimize drug use, receive vocational counseling, and develop new recreational activities and social networks intended to replace those associated with substance use.

Figure 4.6

Community Reinforcement Plus Vouchers Approach to Treating SUD

CRA PLUS VOUCHERS FEATURES:

- Improving family relations, learning skills to reduce drug use, vocational counseling, drug-free recreation and social activities
- Teaching communication, problem solving, and assertiveness skills aimed at increasing satisfaction in nondrinking areas of life
- Antabuse therapy
- Negative cocaine urine tests rewarded with vouchers
- Vouchers exchanged for retail articles

From NIDA, *Principles of Drug Addiction Treatment: A Research-Based Guide.*

2. Patients are taught communication, problem solving, and assertiveness skills aimed at increasing satisfaction in nondrinking areas of life.
3. Those who also abuse alcohol receive clinic-monitored Antabuse therapy.
4. Patients submit urine samples two or three times each week and receive vouchers for cocaine-negative samples.
5. The value of the vouchers increases with consecutive clean samples. Patients may exchange vouchers for retail goods that are consistent with a substance-free lifestyle.

Figure 4.6 provides a synopsis of the community reinforcement plus vouchers approach to treating SUD.

Contingency Management Interventions

Treatment based on contingency management principles has also demonstrated efficacy in the treatment of alcohol, stimulant, opioid, marijuana, and nicotine abuse. It uses the following approach:

> - Patients in drug treatment are given the chance to earn low-cost incentives in exchange for drug-free urine samples.
> - These incentives include prizes given immediately or vouchers exchangeable for food items, movie passes, and other personal goods.

Studies conducted in both methadone programs and psychosocial counseling treatment programs demonstrate that incentive-based interventions are highly effective in increasing treatment retention and in promoting abstinence from drugs.

Figure 4.7 provides a synopsis of the contingency management interventions approach to treating SUD.

Figure 4.7

Contingency Management Interventions Approach to Treating SUD

CONTINGENCY MANAGEMENT FEATURES:

- Earn incentive rewards for drug-free urine tests
- Incentives are immediate prizes and/or vouchers for food, movies, etc.

From NIDA, *Principles of Drug Addiction Treatment: A Research-Based Guide.*

Motivational Enhancement Therapy (MET)

MET is a patient-centered counseling approach for initiating behavior change by help-ing individuals resolve their ambivalence about engaging in treatment and stopping drug use. This approach employs therapeutic techniques, many traditionally associated with nondirective therapies, but is designed to help clients identify and move through the stages of change. It emphasizes enhancement of internally motivated change.

The MET approach is characterized by the following:

➤ The therapy consists of an initial assessment battery session, followed by two to four individual treatment sessions with a therapist.

➤ In the initial treatment session, the therapist provides the client with feedback from the initial assessment battery, stimulating discussion about the client's personal substance use and his or her motivation to change.

➤ Motivational interviewing principles are used to clarify and strengthen motiva-tion, eventually building a plan for change.

➤ Coping strategies for high-risk situations are discussed with the patient.

➤ In subsequent sessions, the therapist monitors change, reviews cessation strat-egies being used, and continues to encourage commitment to change or sus-tained abstinence.

Figure 4.8 provides a synopsis of the motivational enhancement therapy approach to treating SUD.

The Matrix Model

The Matrix Model provides a framework for engaging stimulant abusers in treatment and helping them achieve abstinence. Patients learn about issues critical to add-iction and relapse, receive direction and support from a trained therapist, become familiar with self-help programs, and are monitored for drug use through urine testing.

The therapist functions simultaneously as teacher and coach, fostering a posi-tive, encouraging relationship with the patient and using that relationship to rein-force positive behavior change. The interaction between the therapist and the patient

---

Figure 4.8

Motivational Enhancement Therapy Approach to Treating SUD

MET APPROACH:

- Initial assessment battery
- Assessment feedback and exploring motivation to change
- Motivational interviewing used to clarify and strengthen motivation to implement an action plan
- Coping strategies for cessation developed
- Review of cessation strategies and reinforced commitment to abstinence
- Option to invite significant other to sessions

From NIDA, *Principles of Drug Addiction Treatment: A Research-Based Guide.*

---

is authentic and direct but not confrontational or parental. Therapists are trained to conduct treatment sessions in a way that promotes the patient's self-esteem, dignity, and self-worth. A positive relationship between patient and therapist is critical to patient retention.

Treatment materials for the Matrix Model draw heavily on other tested treatment approaches and, thus, include elements of relapse prevention, family and group therapies, drug education, and self-help participation. Detailed treatment manuals contain worksheets for individual sessions; other components include family education groups, early recovery skills groups, relapse prevention groups, combined sessions, urine tests, 12-step programs, relapse analysis, and social support groups.

Figure 4.9 provides a synopsis of the Matrix Model approach to treating SUD.

Twelve-Step Facilitation Therapy

Twelve-step facilitation therapy is an active engagement intervention designed to increase the likelihood that a substance abuser will become affiliated with and actively involved in 12-step self-help groups and, thus, promote abstinence.

Three key aspects predominate in 12-step facilitation:

- *Acceptance*, which includes the realization that drug addiction is a chronic, progressive disease over which one has no control; that life has become unmanageable because of drugs; that willpower alone is insufficient to overcome the problem; and that abstinence is the only alternative.
- *Surrender*, which involves giving oneself over to a higher power, accepting the fellowship and support structure of other recovering addicted individuals, and following the recovery activities laid out by the 12-step program.
- *Active involvement* in 12-step meetings and related activities.

Figure 4.9

The Matrix Model Approach to Treating SUD

MATRIX MODEL CHARACTERISTICS:

- Urine test monitoring
- Positive, encouraging relationship that reinforces behavior change
- Nonconfrontational, authentic interaction
- Promotion of patient self-esteem and dignity
- Family education
- Drug education
- Self-help group participation
- Relapse prevention skills
- 12-step program participation
- Social support groups

From NIDA, *Principles of Drug Addiction Treatment: A Research-Based Guide.*

Figure 4.10

The 12-Step Facilitation Therapy Approach to Treating SUD

12-STEP FACILITATION ASPECTS:

- Acceptance of addiction as a chronic, progressive disease that takes control of life, making life unmanageable and in need of abstinence
- Surrender of self to a higher power and acknowledgment of the need for support from other addicted individuals in the 12-step program
- Active involvement in 12-step meetings

From NIDA, *Principles of Drug Addiction Treatment: A Research-Based Guide.*

Figure 4.10 provides a synopsis of the 12-step facilitation therapy approach to treating SUD.

Behavioral Couples Therapy (BCT)

BCT is a therapy for alcohol abusers with partners. BCT uses a sobriety/abstinence contract and behavioral principles to reinforce abstinence from drugs and alcohol. Problem-solving and communication skills are taught, and positive interaction activities are promoted. It has been studied as an add-on to individual and group therapy and typically involves 12 weekly couple sessions, lasting approximately 60 minutes each.

Figure 4.11

The Behavioral Couples Therapy Approach to Treating SUD

BEHAVIORAL COUPLES THERAPY FEATURES:

- Sobriety contract signed
- Use of behavioral reinforcement principles to strengthen abstinence
- Problem-solving and communication skills taught
- Positive social interaction promoted
- 12 weekly conjoint sessions

From NIDA, *Principles of Drug Addiction Treatment: A Research-Based Guide*

Figure 4.12

Common Themes of Research-Supported Treatments for Substance Use Disorders

- Establishing a good therapeutic alliance
- Engaging the client in treatment
- Providing incentives for adherence, goal attainment
- Modifying attitudes, behaviors, lifestyle
- Increasing personal skills to identify and manage or avoid high-risk situations
- Enhancing internal motivation
- Enlisting social support

Figure 4.11 provides a synopsis of the behavioral couples therapy approach to treating SUD.

Common Themes of Research-Supported Treatments for Substance Use Disorders

As several reviewers have noted, some themes emerge across these research-supported treatments for substance use disorders that may constitute key areas of therapeutic emphasis. These include establishing a good therapeutic alliance that helps engage people in drug abuse treatment, providing incentives for them to remain adherent to goals, modifying their attitudes and behaviors related to substance use and its role in living a rewarding life, and increasing life skills to handle stressful circumstances as well as environmental cues that may trigger a craving for drugs. Enhancing internal motivation and enlisting social support networks appear to be important in initiating and maintaining therapeutic change.

Key Points

- Several research-supported treatments for SUDs have been identified by multiple independent reviewers.
- Therapist factors and therapeutic relationship factors also appear to be important to achieving a good outcome.
- Common themes across research-supported treatments include:
  - Establishing a good therapeutic alliance
  - Engaging the client in treatment
  - Providing incentives for adherence, goal attainment
  - Modifying attitudes, behaviors, lifestyle
  - Increasing personal skills to identify and manage or avoid high-risk situations
  - Enhancing internal motivation
  - Enlisting social support

Figure 4.12 provides a synopsis of the common themes of research-supported treatments for substance use disorders.

Chapter Review

1. What are the research-supported psychological treatments for SUDs uniformly identified by reviewers of this literature and discussed in this chapter?
2. What are common themes of research-supported treatments for SUDs?

Chapter Review Test Questions

1. Which research-supported treatment for substance use disorders discussed in this chapter focuses primarily on helping individuals resolve their ambivalence about engaging in treatment and stopping substance use?

   A. Behavioral couples therapy
   B. Contingency management
   C. Motivational enhancement therapy
   D. 12-step facilitation

2. In which research-supported treatment approach are patients given the chance to earn low-cost incentives in exchange for clean urine samples?

   A. Behavioral couples therapy
   B. Contingency management
   C. Motivational enhancement therapy
   D. 12-step facilitation therapy

Selected Chapter References

Reviews

Finney, J. W., Wilbourne, P. L., & Moos, R. H. (2007). Psychosocial treatments for substance use disorders. In P. E. Nathan & J. M. Gorman (Eds.), *A Guide to Treatments That Work*. New York, NY: Oxford University Press.

Glasner-Edwards, S., & Rawson, R. A. (2010). Evidence-based practices in addiction treatment: Review and recommendations for public policy. *Health Policy, 97*, 93–104.

National Institute on Drug Abuse. (April 2009). *Principles of drug addiction treatment: A research-based guide* (2nd ed.). Bethesda, MD: National Institute of Health.

National Quality Forum. (September 2007). *National voluntary consensus standards for the treatment of substance use conditions: Evidence-based treatment practices*. Washington, DC: National Quality Forum.

Cognitive–Behavioral Therapy

Empirical Support

Carroll, K. M., Fenton, L. R., Ball, S. A., Nich, C., Frankforter, T. L., Shi, J., & Rounsaville, B. J. (2004). Efficacy of disulfiram and cognitive behavior therapy in cocaine-dependent outpatients: A randomized placebo-controlled trial. *Archives of General Psychiatry, 61*(3), 264–272.

Carroll, K., Rounsaville, B., Nich, C., Gordon, L., Wirtz, P., & Gawin, F. (1994). One-year follow-up of psychotherapy and pharmacotherapy for cocaine dependence: Delayed emergence of psychotherapy effects. *Archives of General Psychiatry, 51*(12), 989–997.

Carroll, K. M., Easton, C. J., Nich, C., Hunkele, K. A., Neavins, T. M., Sinha, R., . . . Rounsaville, B. J. (2006). The use of contingency management and motivational/skills building therapy to treat young adults with marijuana dependence. *Journal of Consulting and Clinical Psychology, 74*, 955–966.

Monti, P. M., & O'Leary, T. A. (1999). Coping and social skills training for alcohol and cocaine dependence. *Psychiatric Clinics of North America, 22*, 447–470.

Monti, P. M., Rohsenow, D. J., Michalec, E., Martin, R. A., & Abrams, D. B. (1997). Brief coping skills treatment for cocaine abuse: Substance use outcomes at 3 months. *Addiction, 92*, 1717–1728.

Project MATCH Research Group. (1997). Matching alcoholism treatments to client heterogeneity: Project MATCH post-treatment drinking outcomes. *Journal of Studies on Alcohol, 58*(1), 7–29.

Clinical Resources

Daley, D. C., & Marlatt, G. A. (2006). *Overcoming your alcohol or drug problem: Effective recovery strategies-therapist guide* (2nd ed.). New York, NY: Oxford University Press.

Epstein, E. E., & McCrady, B. S. (2009). *A cognitive-behavioral treatment program for overcoming alcohol problems: Therapist guide.* New York, NY: Oxford University Press.

Kouimtsidis, C., Reynolds, M., Drummond, C., Davis, P., & Tarrier, N. (2007). *Cognitive behavioural therapy in the treatment of addiction: A treatment planner for clinicians.* London, England: Wiley.

Marlatt, G. A., & Donovan, D. M. (Eds.). (2005). *Relapse prevention: Maintenance strategies in the treatment of addictive behaviors* (2nd ed.). New York, NY: Guilford Press.

Monti, P. M., Abrams, D. B., Kadden, R. M., & Cooney, N. L. (1989). *Treating alcohol dependence: A coping skills training guide.* New York, NY: Guilford Press.

Bibliotherapy Resources

Daley, D. C., & Marlatt, G. A. (2006). *Overcoming your alcohol or drug problem: Effective recovery strategies—Client workbook* (2nd ed.). New York, NY: Oxford University Press.

Epstein, E. E., & McCrady, B. S. (2009). *A cognitive-behavioral treatment program for overcoming alcohol problems—Client workbook.* New York, NY: Oxford University Press.

Training Opportunities

For more information and resources regarding cognitive-behavioral therapy and relapse prevention therapy, see the following clinical guidelines:

Kadden, R. (2001). *Cognitive behavior therapy for substance dependence: Coping skills training. A guideline developed for the Behavioral Health Recovery Management Project.* Available at: http://www.bhrm.org/guidelines/addguidelines.htm

Marlatt, G. A., Parks, G. A., & Witkiewitz, K. (2002). *Clinical guidelines for implementing relapse prevention therapy: A guideline developed for the Behavioral Health Recovery Management Project.* Available at: http://www.bhrm.org/guidelines/addguidelines.htm

Community Reinforcement

Empirical Support

Higgins, S. T., Alessi, S. M., & Dantona, R. L. (2002). Voucher-based contingency management interventions: A substance abuse treatment innovation. *Addictive Behaviors, 27*(6), 887–910.

Higgins, S. T., Sigmon, S. C., Wong, C. J., Heil, S. H., Badger, G. J., Donham, R., . . . Anthony, S. (2003). Community reinforcement therapy for cocaine-dependent outpatients. *Archives of General Psychiatry, 60*, 1043–1052.

Lussier, J. P., Heil, S. H., Mongeon, J. A., Badger, G. J., & Higgins, S. T. (2006). A meta-analysis of voucher-based reinforcement therapy for substance use disorders. *Addiction, 101*, 192–203.

Miller, W. R., Meyers, R. J., Tonigan, J. S., & Grant, K. A. (2001). Community reinforcement and traditional approaches: Findings of a controlled trial. In R. J. Meyers & W. R. Miller (Eds.), *A community reinforcement approach to addiction treatment* (pp. 79–103). New York, NY: Cambridge University Press.

Roozen, H. G., Boulogne, J. J., van Tulder, M. W., van den Brink, W., De Jong, C. A. J., & Kerhof, J. F. M. (2004). A systemic review of the effectiveness of the community reinforcement approach in alcohol, cocaine and opioid addiction. *Drug and Alcohol Dependence, 74*(1), 1–13.

Silverman, K., Higgins, S. T., Brooner, R. K., Montoya, I. D., Cone, E. J., Schuster, C. R., & Preston, K. L. (1996). Sustained cocaine abstinence in methadone maintenance patients through voucher-based reinforcement therapy. *Archives of General Psychiatry, 53*, 409–415.

Smith, J. E., Meyers, R. J., & Delaney, H. D. (1998). The community reinforcement approach with homeless alcohol-dependent individuals. *Journal of Consulting and Clinical Psychology, 66*(3), 541–548.

Stahler, G. J., Shipley, T. E., Kirby, K. C., Godboldte, C., Kerwin, M. E., Shandler, I., & Simons, L. (2005). Development and initial demonstration of a community-based intervention for homeless, cocaine-using, African-American women. *Journal of Substance Abuse Treatment, 28*(2), 171–179.

Clinical Resources

Meyers, R. J., & Miller, W. R. (2006). *A community reinforcement approach to addiction treatment*. Cambridge, England: Cambridge University Press.

Meyers, R. J., & Smith, J. E. (1995). *Clinical guide to alcohol treatment: The community reinforcement approach*. New York, NY: Guilford Press.

Bibliotherapy Resource

Meyers, R. J., & Wolfe, B. L. (2003). *Get your loved one sober: Alternatives to nagging, pleading, and threatening*. Center City, MN: Hazelden.

Training Opportunities

For more information and resources regarding the community reinforcement approach, see the following clinical guideline:

Meyers, R. J., & Squires, D. (2001). *Community reinforcement approach: A guideline developed for the Behavioral Health Recovery Management Project.* Available at: http://www.bhrm.org/guidelines/addguidelines.htm

For more information about training opportunities, contact:

Robert J. Meyers, Ph.D., UNM Center on Alcoholism, Substance Abuse and Addictions (CASAA), 2350 Alamo SE, Bldg. 2, Albuquerque, NM 87106; bmeyers@unm.edu.

Jane Ellen Smith, Ph.D., Department of Psychology, Logan Hall, University of New Mexico, Albuquerque, NM 87131; janellen@unm.edu.

Contingency Management

Empirical Support

Budney, A. J., Moore, B. A., Rocha, H. L., & Higgins, S. T. (2006). Clinical trial of abstinence-based vouchers and cognitive-behavioral therapy for cannabis dependence. *Journal of Consulting and Clinical Psychology, 74*(2), 307–316.

Higgins, S. T., Alessi, S. M., & Dantona, R. L. (2002). Voucher-based contingency management interventions: A substance abuse treatment innovation. *Addictive Behaviors, 27*(6), 887–910.

Lussier, J. P., Heil, S. H., Mongeon, J. A., Badger, G. J., & Higgins, S. T. (2006). A meta-analysis of voucher-based reinforcement therapy for substance use disorders. *Addiction, 101*, 192–203.

Peirce, J. M., Petry, N. M., Stitzer, M. L., Blaine, J., Kellogg, S., Satterfield, F., . . . Li, R. (2006). Effects of lower-cost incentives on stimulant abstinence in methadone maintenance treatment: A National Drug Abuse Treatment Clinical Trials Network study. *Archives of General Psychiatry, 63*(2), 201–208.

Petry, N. M., Peirce, J. M., Sitizer, M. L., Blaine, J., Roll, J. M., Cohen, A., . . . Li, R. (2005). Prize-based incentives increase retention in outpatient psychosocial treatment programs: Results of the National Drug Abuse Treatment Clinical Trials Network Study. *Archives of General Psychiatry, 62*, 1148–1156.

Prendergast, M., Podus, D., Finney, J., Greenwell, L., & Roll, J. (2006). Contingency management for treatment of substance use disorders: A meta-analysis. *Addiction, 101*, 1546–1560.

Roll, J. M., Petry, N. M., Sitizer, M. L., Brecht, M. L., Peirce, J. M., McCann, M. J., . . . Kellogg, S. (2006). Contingency management for the treatment of methamphetamine use disorders. *The American Journal of Psychiatry, 163*(11), 1993–1999.

Clinical Resources

Henggeler, S. W., Cunningham, P. B., Rowland, M. D., & Schoenwald, S. K. (2011). *Contingency management for adolescent substance abuse.* New York, NY: Guilford Press.

Higgins, S. T., Silverman, K., & Heil, S. H. (Eds.). (2007). *Contingency management in substance abuse treatment.* New York, NY: Guilford Press.

Petry, N. M. (2011). *Contingency management for substance abuse treatment: A guide to implementing this evidence-based practice.* New York, NY: Routledge.

Bibliotherapy Resources and Training Opportunities

For more information and resources regarding contingency management, see the following clinical guideline:

Petry, N. M. (2001). *A clinician's guide for implementing contingency management programs: A guideline developed for the Behavioral Health Recovery Management Project.* Available at: http://www.bhrm.org/guidelines/addguidelines.htm.

For more resources on contingency management, see the University of Connecticut Health Center Contingency Management Program Web site at http://contingency management.uchc.edu/who/index.html.

Motivational Enhancement Therapy/Motivational Interviewing

Empirical Support

Baker, A., Lewin, T., Reichler, H., Clancy, R., Carr, V., Garrett, R., Sly, K., . . . Terry. M, (2002). Evaluation of a motivational interview for substance use within psychiatric in-patient services. *Addiction, 97,* 1329–1337.

Ball, S. A., Martino, S., Nich, C., Frankforter, T. L., van Horn, D., Crits-Christoph, P., . . . Carroll, K. M. (2007). Site matters: Multisite randomized trial of motivational enhancement therapy in community drug abuse clinics. *Journal of Consulting and Clinical Psychology, 75*(4), 556–567.

Becker, S. J., & Curry, J. F. (2008). Outpatient interventions for adolescent substance abuse: A quality of evidence review. *Journal of Consulting and Clinical Psychology, 76,* 531–544.

Brown, J. M., & Miller, W. R. (1993). Impact of motivational interviewing on participation and outcome in residential alcoholism treatment. *Psychology of Addictive Behaviors, 7,* 211–218.

Haug, N. A., Svikis, D. S., & DiClemente, C. (2004). Motivational enhancement therapy for nicotine dependence in methadone-maintained pregnant women. *Psychology of Addictive Behaviors, 18*(3), 289–292.

Hettema, J., Steele, J., & Miller, W. R. (2005). Motivational interviewing. *Annual Review of Clinical Psychology, 1,* 91–111.

Lundahl, B. W., Kunz, C., Brownell, C., Tollefson, D., & Burke, B. L. (2010). A meta-analysis of motivational interviewing: Twenty-five years of empirical studies. *Research on Social Work Practice, 20*(2), 137–160.

Marijuana Treatment Project Research Group. (2004). Brief treatments for cannabis dependence: Findings from a randomized multisite trial. *Journal of Consulting and Clinical Psychology, 72*(3), 455–466.

Miller, W. R., Benefield, G., & Tonigan, J. S. (1993). Enhancing motivation for change in problem drinking: A controlled comparison of two therapist styles. *Journal of Consulting and Clinical Psychology, 61*(3), 455–461.

Miller, W. R., Yahne, C. E., & Tonigan, J. S. (2003). Motivational interviewing in drug abuse services: A randomized trial. *Journal of Consulting and Clinical Psychology, 71*(4), 754–763.

Project MATCH Research Group. (1997). Matching alcoholism treatments to client heterogeneity: Project MATCH post-treatment drinking outcomes. *Journal of Studies on Alcohol, 58*(1), 7–29.

Stephens, R. S., Roffman, R. A., & Curtin, L. (2000). Comparison of extended versus brief treatments for marijuana use. *Journal of Consulting and Clinical Psychology, 68*(5), 898–908.

Stotts, A. L., DiClemente, C. C., & Dolan-Mullen, P. (2002). One-to-one: A motivational intervention for resistant pregnant smokers. *Addictive Behaviors, 27*(2), 275–292.

UKATT Research Team. (2005). Effectiveness of treatment for alcohol problems: Findings of the randomised UK alcohol treatment trial (UKATT). *British Medical Journal, 331,* 541–544.

Waldron, H. B., & Turner, C. W. (2008). Evidence-based psychosocial treatments for adolescent substance abuse. *Journal of Clinical Child & Adolescent Psychology, 37,* 238–261.

Clinical Resources, Bibliotherapy Resources, and Training Opportunities

For more information and resources regarding motivational interviewing, see the following clinical guideline:

Squires, D., & Moyers, T. (2001). *Motivational interviewing: A guideline developed for the Behavioral Health Recovery Management Project.* Available at: http://www.bhrm.org/guidelines/addguidelines.htm

For more information on motivational enhancement therapy and motivational interviewing resources, see the Motivational Interviewing Web site at http://www.motivationalinterview.org/

The Matrix Model

Empirical Support

Huber, A., Ling, W., Shoptaw, S., Gulati, V., Brethen, P., & Rawson, R. (1997). Integrating treatments for methamphetamine abuse: A psychosocial perspective. *Journal of Addictive Diseases, 16*(4), 41–50.

Rawson, R., Shoptaw, S., Obert, J. L., McCann, M., Hasson, A., Marinelli-Casey, P., . . . Ling, W. (1995). An intensive outpatient approach for cocaine abuse: The Matrix Model. *Journal of Substance Abuse Treatment, 12*(2), 117–127.

Rawson, R. A., Huber, A., McCann, M. J., Shoptaw, S., Farabee, D., Reiber, C., & Ling, W. (2002). A comparison of contingency management and cognitive-behavioral approaches during methadone maintenance treatment for cocaine dependence. *Archives of General Psychiatry, 59*, 817–824.

Rawson, R. A., Marinelli-Casey, P., Anglin, M. D., Dickow, A., Frazier, Y., Gallagher, C., . . . Zweben, J. (2004). A multi-site comparison of psychosocial approaches for the treatment of methamphetamine dependence. *Addiction, 99*, 708–717.

Shoptaw, S., Rawson, R. A., McCann, M. J., & Obert, J. L. (1994). The Matrix Model of stimulant abuse treatment: Evidence of efficacy. *Journal of Addictive Diseases, 13*, 129–141.

Clinical Resources, Bibliotherapy Resources, and Training Opportunities

For more information and resources regarding the Matrix Model, see the following clinical guideline:

Rawson, R. A. (2006). The Matrix Model of intensive outpatient treatment: *A guideline developed for the Behavioral Health Recovery Management Project.* Available at: http://www.bhrm.org/guidelines/addguidelines.htm

For more information on the Matrix Model resources, see the Matrix Institute on Addictions Web site at http://www.matrixinstitute.org/index.html

12–Step Facilitation

Empirical Support

Carroll, K. M., Nich, C., Ball, S. A., McCance, E., Frankforter, T. L., & Rounsaville, B. J. (2000). One-year follow-up of disulfiram and psychotherapy for cocaine-alcohol users: Sustained effects of treatment. *Addiction, 95*(9), 1335–1349.

Donovan, D. M., & Wells, E. A. (2007). Tweaking 12-step: The potential role of 12-step self-help group involvement in methamphetamine recovery. *Addiction, 102*(Suppl. 1), 121–129.

Longabaugh, R., Wirtz, P. W., Zweben, A., & Stout, R. L. (1998). Network support for drinking, Alcoholics Anonymous and long-term matching effects. *Addiction, 93*(9), 1313–1333.

Ouimette, P. C., Moos, R., & Finney, J. (1998). Influence of outpatient treatment and 12-step group involvement on one-year substance abuse treatment outcomes. *Journal of Studies on Alcohol, 59*, 513–522.

Project MATCH Research Group. (1997). Matching alcoholism treatments to client heterogeneity: Project MATCH posttreatment drinking outcomes. *Journal of Studies on Alcohol, 58*(1), 7–29.

Project MATCH Research Group. (1998). Matching alcoholism treatments to client heterogeneity: Project MATCH three-year drinking outcomes. *Alcoholism: Clinical and Experimental Research, 22,* 1300–1311

Clinical Resources, Bibliotherapy Resources, and Training Opportunities

For more information and resources regarding 12-step facilitation, see the Hazelden Web site at http://www.hazelden.org/

Behavioral Couples Therapy

Empirical Support

Fals-Stewart, W., Birchler, G. R., & Kelley, M. L. (2006). Learning sobriety together: A randomized clinical trial examining behavioral couples therapy with alcoholic female patients. *Journal of Consulting and Clinical Psychology, 74,* 579–591.

Fals-Stewart, W., Birchler, G. R., & O'Farrell, T. J. (1996). Behavioral couples therapy for male substance-abusing patients: Effects on relationship adjustment and drug-using behavior. *Journal of Consulting and Clinical Psychology, 64,* 959–972.

Fals-Stewart, W., Kashdan, T. B., O'Farrell, T. J., & Birchler, G. R. (2002). Behavioral couples therapy for drug-abusing patients: Effects on partner violence. *Journal of Substance Abuse Treatment, 22,* 87–96.

Fals-Stewart, W., Klostermann, K., Yates, B. T., O'Farrell, T. J., & Birchler, G. R. (2005). Brief relationship therapy for alcoholism: A randomized clinical trial examining clinical efficacy and cost-effectiveness. *Psychology of Addictive Behaviors, 19,* 363–371.

Fals-Stewart, W., & O'Farrell, T. J. (2003). Behavioral family counseling and naltrexone for male opioid-dependent patients. *Journal of Consulting and Clinical Psychology, 71,* 432–442.

Fals-Stewart, W., O'Farrell, T. J., & Birchler, G. R. (2001). Behavioral couples therapy for male methadone maintenance patients: Effects on drug-using behavior and relationship adjustment. *Behavior Therapy, 32,* 391–411.

Fals-Stewart, W., O'Farrell, T. J., Feehan, M., Birchler, G. R., Tiller, S., & McFarlin, S. K. (2000). Behavioral couples therapy versus individual-based treatment for male substance-abusing patients. An evaluation of significant individual change and comparison of improvement rates. *Journal of Substance Abuse Treatment, 18,* 249–254.

Kelley, M. L., & Fals-Stewart, W. (2002). Couples- versus individual-based therapy for alcohol and drug abuse: Effects on children's psychosocial functioning. *Journal of Consulting and Clinical Psychology, 70,* 417–427.

O'Farrell, T. J., Murphy, C. M., Stephan, S. H., Fals-Stewart, W., & Murphy, M. (2004). Partner violence before and after couples-based alcoholism treatment for male alcoholic patients: The role of treatment involvement and abstinence. *Journal of Consulting and Clinical Psychology, 72*, 202–217.

Winters, J., Fals-Stewart, W., O'Farrell, T. J., Birchler, G. R., & Kelley, M. L. (2002). Behavioral couples therapy for female substance-abusing patients: Effects on substance use and relationship adjustment. *Journal of Consulting and Clinical Psychology, 70*, 344–355.

Clinical Resources

Fals-Stewart, W., O'Farrell, T., Birchler, G., & Gorman, C. (2006). *Behavioral couples therapy for drug abuse and alcoholism: A 12-session manual* (2nd ed.). Buffalo, NY: Addiction and Family Research Group.

O'Farrell, T. J., & Fals-Stewart, W. (2006). *Behavioral couples therapy for alcoholism and drug abuse*. New York, NY: Guilford Press.

Bibliotherapy Resources and Training Opportunities

For more information and resources regarding behavioral couples therapy, see the following clinical guideline:

O'Farrell, T. J., & Fals-Stewart, W. (2002). *Behavioral couples therapy for alcoholism and drug abuse: A guideline developed for the Behavioral Health Recovery Management Project.* Available at: www.bhrm.org/guidelines/addguidelines.htm

A Web-based distance learning course on behavioral couples therapy is available at: www.ireta.org/ireta_main/distance_learning.ht

For more information on behavioral couples therapy, contact the Harvard Families and Addiction Research Program at http://www.hms.harvard.edu/psych/redbook/redbook-addictions-07.htm

Note: Training opportunities information is from www.psychologicaltreatments.org.

5

How Do You Integrate Empirically Supported Treatments Into Treatment Planning?

Construction of an empirically informed treatment plan for Substance Use Disorder (SUD) involves integrating objectives and treatment interventions consistent with identified empirically supported treatments (ESTs) into a client's treatment plan, after you have determined that the client's primary problem fits those described in the target population of the EST research. Of course, implementing ESTs must be done in consideration of important client, therapist, and therapeutic relationship factors—consistent with APA's definition of evidence-based practice.

Definitions

The behavioral definition statements describe *how the problem manifests itself in the client*. Although there are several common features of SUD, the behavioral definition of SUD for your client will be unique and specific to him or her. Your assessment will need to identify which features best characterize your client's presentation. Accordingly, the *behavioral definition* of your treatment plan is tailored to your individual client's clinical picture. When the primary problem reflects a recognized psychiatric diagnosis, the behavioral definition statements are usually closely aligned with diagnostic criteria such as those provided in the *DSM* or *ICD*. Examples of common SUD definition statements are the following:

- ➤ Displays a maladaptive pattern of substance use, leading to clinically significant impairment or distress.
- ➤ Demonstrates increased tolerance for the drug, as there is the need to use more to become intoxicated or a markedly diminished effect with continued use of the same amount of the substance.
- ➤ Exhibits physical withdrawal symptoms (e.g., shaking, seizures, nausea, headaches, sweating) when going without the substance for any length of time, or a substance is taken to relieve or avoid withdrawal symptoms.

➤ Fails to stop or cut down use of mood-altering drug once started, despite the verbalized desire to do so and the negative consequences continued use brings.

➤ Takes the substance in larger amounts or over a longer period than was intended.

➤ Demonstrates a great deal of time spent in activities necessary to obtain the substance, use the substance, or recover from its effects.

➤ Reports suspension of important social or occupational role obligations because they interfere with using.

➤ Evidences recurrent use in situations in which it is physically hazardous.

➤ Exhibits recurrent substance-related legal problems.

➤ Continues substance use despite experiencing persistent physical, financial, vocational, social, and/or relationship problems that are directly caused by the use of the substance.

➤ The symptoms have never met the criteria for Substance Dependence for this class of substance.

The list begins with statements descriptive of substance dependence, such as those that summarize the symptoms of tolerance, withdrawal, and compulsive substance use. Statements descriptive of substance abuse share some of the criteria with substance dependence. The last statement is reserved for a client struggling with the less severe problem of substance abuse.

Goals

Goals are broad statements describing what you and the client would like the result of therapy to be. One statement may suffice, but more than one can be used in the treatment plan. Examples of common goal statements for SUD are the following:

➤ Accept the unmanageability over mood-altering substances, and participate in a recovery-based program.

➤ Establish a sustained recovery, free from the use of all mood-altering substances.

➤ Establish and maintain total abstinence, while increasing knowledge of the disease and the process of recovery.

➤ Acquire the necessary 12-step skills to maintain long-term sobriety from all mood-altering substances, and live a life free of substance abuse.

➤ Improve quality of life by maintaining an ongoing abstinence from all mood-altering chemicals.

Objectives and Interventions

Objectives are statements that describe *small, observable steps the client must achieve* toward attaining the goal of successful treatment. Intervention statements describe the *actions taken by the therapist* to assist the client in achieving his/her objectives. Each objective must be paired with at least one intervention.

Assessment

All approaches to quality treatment start with a thorough assessment of the nature and history of the client's presenting problems. EST approaches rely on a thorough psychosocial assessment of the nature, history, and severity of the problem as experienced by the client.

Our list of objective statements begins with one describing client cooperation with a medical assessment to evaluate the possible negative physical effects of his or her substance abuse. Interventions one and two for this objective call for the therapist to refer the client for this medical evaluation and an assessment for the need for psychotropic medication treatment. If medications are prescribed, the client should be monitored for his or her compliance with the prescription as well as for the effectiveness and side effects of the medication.

The assessment should also track the client's possible withdrawal symptoms that may need medical attention. Objective instruments, such as the SASSI-3, may be administered to assess the client's substance use patterns and their effects. Finally, objective number five describes the thorough substance use biopsychosocial history that must be gathered from the client and may include family members and others.

Table 5.1 contains examples of assessment objectives and interventions for SUD.

Psychoeducation

A common feature of many ESTs for SUD is initial and ongoing psychoeducation. Common emphases include helping the client learn about SUD, the treatment, and its rationale. Books or other educational materials are often recommended to the client to supplement psychoeducation done in session. It is important to instill hope in the client and have them on board as a partner in the treatment process. With ESTs, discussing their demonstrated efficacy with the client may facilitate this process.

We have written three objectives to capture common psychoeducational processes and themes. The client is given information about addiction and the treatment through didactic group meetings, assigned readings, and individual review of new information and how it applies to the client specifically. Within group and individual sessions, the client is encouraged to talk about how the addiction has affected his or her life, specifically listing the negative consequences that have accrued resulting from the substance use.

Table 5.1   Assessment Objectives and Interventions

Objectives	Interventions
1. Cooperate with medical assessment and an evaluation of the necessity for pharmacological intervention.	1. Refer the client to a medical healthcare provider to perform an assessment of possible medical effects of substance use, assess the need for psychotropic medication for any mental/emotional comorbidities, and discuss the use of acamprosate (Campral), naltrexone (Vivitrol), or disulfiram (Antabuse) where applicable. 2. Refer the client to a pharmacology-based treatment/ recovery program (e.g., acamprosate, naltrexone), where applicable.
2. Take prescribed medications as directed by the physician.	1. Physician will monitor the effectiveness and side effects of medication, titrating as necessary. 2. Monitor psychotropic medication prescription for compliance, effectiveness, and side effects.
3. Report acute withdrawal symptoms to the staff.	1. Assess and monitor the client's condition during withdrawal, using a standardized procedure (e.g., Narcotic Withdrawal Scale) as needed.
4. Complete psychological testing or objective questionnaires for assessing substance dependence.	1. Administer to the client psychological instruments designed to objectively assess substance dependence (e.g., Substance Use Disorders Diagnostic Schedule-IV [SUDDS-IV], Substance Abuse Subtle Screen Inventory-3 [SASSI-3]); give the client feedback regarding the results of the assessment; readminister as needed to assess outcome.
5. Provide honest and complete information for a chemical dependence biopsychosocial history.	1. Complete a thorough family and personal biopsychosocial history that has a focus on addiction (e.g., family history of addiction and treatment, other substances used, progression of substance abuse, consequences of abuse).

Key Points

COMMON EMPHASES OF INITIAL PSYCHOEDUCATION INCLUDE:

- Teaching the client about the nature and etiology of the diagnosed condition
- Informing the client regarding the various treatment options consistent with the best available evidence
- Explaining the rationale for the treatment approach that will be used
- Utilizing reading assignments as homework, if needed, to facilitate understanding of psychoeducational goals

Table 5.2 contains examples of psychoeducational objectives and interventions for SUD.

Table 5.2   Psychoeducation Objectives and Interventions

Objectives	Interventions
6. Attend didactic sessions and read assigned material in order to increase knowledge of addiction and the process of recovery.	1. Assign the client to attend a chemical dependence didactic series to increase his/her knowledge of the patterns and effects of chemical dependence; ask him/her to identify several key points attained from each didactic series and process these points with the therapist. 2. Assign the client to read a workbook describing evidence-based treatment approaches to addiction recovery (e.g., *Overcoming Your Alcohol or Drug Problem*, 2nd ed., by Daley and Marlatt); use the readings to reinforce key concepts and practices throughout therapy. 3. Assign the client to read material on addiction (e.g., *Willpower's Not Enough* by Washton; *The Addiction Workbook* by Fanning; or *Alcoholics Anonymous*); process key points gained from the reading. 4. Assign the client to read the book *Narcotics Anonymous* and gather five key points from it to process with the therapist.
7. Attend group therapy sessions to learn more about addiction and share thoughts and feelings associated with, reasons for, consequences of, feelings about, and alternatives to addiction.	1. Assign the client to attend group therapy. 2. Direct group therapy that facilitates the client's understanding of addiction as well as his/her sharing of causes for, consequences of, feelings about, and alternatives to addiction.
8. List and discuss negative consequences resulting from or exacerbated by substance dependence.	1. Ask the client to make a list of the ways chemical use has negatively impacted his/her life (or assign "Substance Abuse Negative Impact Versus Sobriety's Positive Impact" in the *Adult Psychotherapy Homework Planner*, 2nd ed., by Jongsma); process the list in individual or group sessions. 2. Use reflection to highlight the client's use of denial to minimize the severity of and negative consequences of substance abuse. 3. Using the biopsychosocial history and client's list of negative consequences of substance abuse, assist him/her in understanding the need to stay in treatment.

Assessment/Psychoeducation Review

1. What are common emphases of initial psychoeducation?

Assessment/Psychoeducation Review Test Questions

1. At what point in therapy is psychoeducation conducted?

   A. At the end of therapy
   B. During the assessment phase
   C. During the initial treatment session
   D. Throughout therapy

Motivational Enhancement Therapy

Our next set of objectives and interventions reflects use of motivational enhancement therapy. Statements 9 and 10 summarize the client's objectives for this approach. The therapist interventions for objective 9 describe the client-centered, empathic style of this therapy, in which the therapist establishes rapport and uses motivational interviewing to explore the client's motivation for change. As discrepancies between the client's current behavior and desired life goals become evident, the therapist highlights these without direct confrontation. Objective 10 and its associated intervention describe the goal of attaining client commitment to an action plan for termination of substance use.

Key Points

KEY CHARACTERISTICS OF MOTIVATIONAL ENHANCEMENT THERAPY

- The therapy involves an initial assessment battery session, followed by two to four individual treatment sessions with a therapist.
- In the initial treatment session, the therapist provides the client feedback from the initial assessment battery, stimulating discussion about the client's personal substance use and his or her motivation to change.
- Motivational interviewing principles are used to clarify and strengthen motivation, eventually building a plan for change.
- Coping strategies for high-risk situations are often discussed with the patient.
- In subsequent sessions, the therapist monitors change, reviews cessation strategies being used, and continues to encourage commitment to change or sustained abstinence.

Table 5.3 contains examples of objectives and interventions consistent with Motivational Enhancement Therapy for SUD.

Table 5.3   Motivational Enhancement Therapy Objectives and Interventions

Objectives	Interventions
9. Explore and resolve ambivalence associated with commitment to change behaviors related to substance use and addiction.	1. Using a directive, client-centered, empathic style derived from motivational enhancement therapy (see *Motivational Interviewing* by Miller and Rollnick; and *Addiction and Change* by DiClemente), establish rapport with the client and listen reflectively, asking permission before providing information or advice. 2. Ask open-ended questions to explore the client's own motivations for change, affirming his/her change-related statements and efforts (see *Substance Abuse Treatment and the Stages of Change* by Connors, Donovan, and DiClemente). 3. Elicit recognition of the discrepancy gap between current behavior and desired life goals, reflecting resistance without direct confrontation or argumentation.
10. Commit self to an action plan directed toward termination of substance use.	1. Encourage and support the client's self-efficacy for change toward the goal of developing an action plan for termination of substance use to which the client is willing to commit.

Demonstration Vignette

Motivational Enhancement Therapy

Here we present the transcript of the dialogue depicted in the Motivational Enhancement Therapy vignette.

Therapist: I appreciate you giving me the information on your drinking habits, Brian. Did you get a chance to see the feedback sheet I prepared for you and your wife?

Client: Yeah, I read it.

Therapist: What are your thoughts on it?

Client: Well, I was surprised to see that I drink more than, what, 85 percent of people?

Therapist: Yeah, based on a comparison to the population in general.

Client: I knew I drank, but I didn't know how it compared. [looks a little irritable]

Therapist: You look bothered by that.

Client: Well, I don't like it, but how do you know if the rest of the country just doesn't drink much. I mean, maybe they just don't drink at all. It doesn't necessarily mean it's bad.

Therapist: That's true. It just says that 85 percent drink less. It doesn't say anything about whether that's bad.

Client: Yeah, well, I'm sure it's not good.

Therapist: So seeing how much you drink in comparison to others doesn't mean it's bad, but you also feel like it probably is for other reasons?

Client: I don't know. Some of the other stuff on the sheet kinda got me.

Therapist: What stuff hit you like that?

Client: [pauses] Well, I didn't realize that my wife felt the way she did about it. You know, she's never said anything like that to me before. She's just pretty much been angry.

Therapist: She hasn't voiced this other stuff to you before? What did she say that hit you so hard?

Client: [pauses] The stuff about losing me, losing the guy she married. [chokes up a bit]

Therapist: I can see it upsets you. How does it make you feel?

Client: Ashamed. Like I'm not the guy she married anymore.

Therapist: Being the guy she married is obviously important to you.

Client: Of course it is. It used to be. I'm not so sure about that now.

Therapist: You don't know if it's important anymore?

Client: No, it is. I mean I'm just not that guy anymore. I've changed.

Therapist: It's important to you to be that guy, but you're struggling to be that guy now?

Client: Yeah. I mean I used to be the strong one, the go-getter, the "we can do anything guy," you know what I mean?

Therapist: I do. Why aren't you that way now?

Client: Drinking. I pretty much check out with the drinking.

Therapist: You seem disappointed.

Client: Yeah, in myself.

Therapist: Brian, sometimes our motivation to get things back comes from the negatives that happen to others as a result of our drinking. This one seems important to you.

Client: It is. I don't like this part of it. I don't like disappointing her like this.

Therapist: I can see that. When we first talked about looking at these consequences, positive and negative, we said that we might keep the ones that meant a lot, separate them out. Is this one of them?

Client: Yeah. When I think of this, it makes me want to change, get back to what I was.

Therapist: Okay, I'll put this one aside. How about we go over the rest of this sheet the same way? See what we find?

Client: Boy, that sounds like fun. [sarcastic, but not hostile]

Therapist: I know. You don't have to if you don't want to. These are your decisions.

(continued)

Client:	No, I don't mean it. We probably should.
Therapist:	All right. You had mentioned some possible positive consequences to quitting. Which ones come to mind now?
Client:	Well, I feel crappy most of the time. I think quitting would probably help me feel better. I mean, the only time I feel good is when I first start drinking. The rest of the time I'm dead. I'm tired all the time, strung out.
Therapist:	You'd indicated some concerns about your health.
Client:	I'm starting to wonder about it, but I haven't gone to the doctor because I'm afraid of what he might tell me.
Therapist:	What concerns do you have?
Client:	Well, I know I've gained weight, and that's not good. I also don't have the stamina I used to have. I wonder about how drinking is affecting my heart and my liver. And then there are the stomach pains that come and go, and I wonder if that is related to something serious from my drinking. So, do you think I should just go to the doctor, just get the answers?
Therapist:	It sounds like you know you should go to the doctor.
Client:	Yeah.
Therapist:	So, if I am hearing you accurately, Brian, getting your wife's faith in you restored and improving your health are two results of sobriety that motivate you to try to succeed in your recovery. Is that right?
Client:	Yes.
Therapist:	What other positive effects of maintaining sobriety might help you stay on course?

Critique of the Motivational Enhancement Therapy Demonstration Vignette

The following points were made in the critique:

a. The session is built around a review of an assessment form the client and his wife had completed previously; the form collects information about the client's substance abuse and its consequences for himself and significant others.

b. Therapist is using reflective techniques to help the client clarify his thoughts and feelings and bring out points of conflict between the client's lifestyle and his wishes that could serve to motivate change.

c. Therapist focuses on the client's wife's disappointment in him and the client's health concerns as issues that could motivate him toward action for change.

Additional points that could be made:

a. Decisions for continuing the direction of the session are left to the client; this is a client-centered approach.

b. Client acknowledges that his drinking pattern is "not good" as he develops insight without confrontation.

Comments you would like to make:

_____

_____

_____

_____

Homework: The exercise "Problem Identification" (_Addiction Treatment Homework Planner_, 4th ed., by Finley and Lenz) is designed to allow the client to discover his/her personal losses and problems associated with addictive behaviors. This will contribute to the client's motivation to change and lead to an action plan. The assignment "Alternatives to Addictive Behavior" (Finley and Lenz) strengthens the motivation to change by identifying positive ways to get personal needs met without using (see www.wiley.com/go/sudwb).

Motivational Enhancement Therapy Review

1. What are key characteristics of motivational enhancement therapy?

Motivational Enhancement Therapy Review Test Question

1. Although using techniques most associated with nondirective therapies, motivational enhancement therapy is guided by which of the following goals?

    A. To confront clients about the negative consequences of their substance use
    B. To help clients understand the developmental origins of their substance use
    C. To improve clients' understanding of the negative consequences of their substance use
    D. To move clients through the stages of change toward action

Community Reinforcement Approach

Our next research-supported treatment is the community reinforcement approach. Objectives 11 through 14 capture major emphases of this approach. The statements start with the client taking The Happiness Scale and being given feedback about the results. Therapeutic goals are developed, with a focus on increasing satisfaction in nondrinking aspects of life. This treatment approach also places emphasis on teaching the client life skills such as communication, problem-solving, and assertiveness skills aimed at increasing satisfaction in nondrinking areas of life, as well as effective personal and interpersonal functioning. Homework assignments may be given to strengthen newly learned behavioral skills. A relapse prevention plan is also commonly developed.

To broaden the client's focus on finding satisfaction apart from drinking activities, the therapist may teach skills necessary for finding or maintaining employment. The therapist may also attempt to help the client identify new areas of recreation and social relationships where satisfaction may be found without substance use.

Finally, conjoint sessions may be held to address and resolve relationship issues with the partner and to increase the frequency of their pleasant interactions.

Key Points

CHARACTERISTICS OF THE COMMUNITY REINFORCEMENT APPROACH

- The community reinforcement approach is a comprehensive behavioral program for treating substance abuse problems.
- It is based on the belief that environmental contingencies can play a powerful role in encouraging or discouraging drinking or drug use.
- It utilizes social, recreational, familial, and vocational reinforcers to replace those provided by substance use.
- It teaches life skills to improve personal and interpersonal effectiveness.
- A primary goal of the approach is to make a sober lifestyle more rewarding than the use of substances.

Table 5.4 contains examples of objectives and interventions for the community reinforcement approach for SUD.

Table 5.4   Community Reinforcement Approach Objectives and Interventions

Objectives	Interventions
11. Identify level of happiness in various areas of life.	1. Approaching the client with empathy and genuine caring, administer The Happiness Scale (see *A Community Reinforcement Approach to Addiction Treatment* by Meyers & Miller); review results in session.
12. Develop goals to increase satisfaction and pleasure in unsatisfactory, nondrinking areas of life.	1. Using the Goals of Counseling chart, assist the client in defining specific goals and strategies for achieving goals for increased happiness in problematic, nondrinking areas of life, so that the role of alcohol and/or drugs as the major determinant of an individual's happiness is diminished.
13. Learn and implement communication, problem-solving, and assertiveness skills toward achieving goals.	1. Using modeling, role-playing, and behavioral rehearsal, teach the client communication skills, including how to make statements that convey understanding, accepting partial responsibility for problems, and offering to help solve the problem.

Objectives	Interventions
	2. Teach the client problem-solving skills (identify and pinpoint the problem, brainstorm possible solutions, list and evaluate the pros and cons of each solution, select and implement a solution, evaluate all parties' satisfaction with the action, adjust action if necessary); use role-playing to assist the client in applying these steps to life issues to increase happiness.
	3. Teach the client assertiveness skills that can be used to support drink refusal.
	4. Assign homework to encourage the client to apply the newly learned behavioral skills to achieving the happiness goals identified; review progress, reinforcing success and redirecting for failure.
	5. Develop a relapse prevention action plan to address high-risk trigger situations that can lead to a return to substance use.
14. Cooperate with exploration of increasing satisfaction in areas of life that can support sobriety, such as employment, recreation, and relationships.	1. Teach the client skills necessary for finding a job, keeping a job, and improving satisfaction in a job setting.
	2. Assist the client in identifying new sources of nondrinking recreation and social friendships, using problem-solving and communication skills to overcome obstacles.
	3. Direct conjoint sessions that address and resolve issues with a partner so as to increase the number of pleasant interactions and reduce conflicts.

Demonstration Vignette

Community Reinforcement Approach

Here we present the transcript of the dialogue depicted in the Community Reinforcement Approach vignette.

Therapist: Hi, Brian. Last time we met, you identified one of your goals as finding more interesting and fun things to do that don't involve drinking or using drugs.

(continued)

Client: Yeah, I think I need to do that more.

Therapist: Good. This is a great goal, because we know that finding ways to get the positives out of life that don't involve substance use can help you in getting sober and staying sober.

Client: That makes sense. I've been sober for about three weeks now, and to be honest, I'm finding it difficult to fill my time. I never realized how much time I spent drinking.

Therapist: It's a big change, and I can imagine that if you're having trouble finding other things to do, you might start thinking about drinking?

Client: Oh yeah, that's when it's really hard. My cravings get really strong.

Therapist: Well, you're doing a fantastic job managing those cravings! But we definitely want to start getting you involved in some rewarding activities so it's not such a daily struggle.

Client: Sounds good to me.

Therapist: Okay, on the form you filled out, you checked some possible activities that you've done at least once in the past few months and found enjoyable. Any of those come to mind now?

Client: Yeah, I've been thinking about it. I like bowling a lot. I like the game, the atmosphere. I think that could be one.

Therapist: Good. Now one thing we need to consider is whether this activity is highly associated with drinking. Did you drink while you bowled?

Client: [Laughs] Yeah, I sure did. So maybe that's not such a good activity?

Therapist: Probably not now. At this stage we don't want to choose things that are likely to trigger you to drink. Are there any other activities that you used to like that don't involve alcohol?

Client: Boy, this isn't easy. Most things I did for the past few years always involved drinking [thinks hard]. Well, I don't know if this counts, but I did used to like to go hiking. I haven't done it in awhile, but I did enjoy it, and I didn't drink when I did that.

Therapist: That sounds perfect! Now you said you haven't done it in awhile?

Client: Yeah. I don't know, it's like I enjoy it but yet I just can't seem to motivate myself to do it.

Therapist: Well, today we are going to look at what might make it easier for you to do it. We're going to do something called "functional analysis." It is a fancy name for just looking at things you could do to make it more likely that you will actually go hiking. It'll also help us to see whether hiking is likely to give you some of the rewards that alcohol used to give you.

Client: Hiking will get me drunk?

Therapist: Well, not in that way, but let's see what it does for you. You've said that one of the things you liked about drinking is that it helped you to relax and forget about the worries of the day. Does hiking help you relax and forget your worries?

Client: I see where you are going. Yeah, I guess it did, in a different way, but it could.

Therapist: Then we already know one benefit you're likely to get from hiking! Let's explore this more. I'm going to ask you some questions about how you like to hike, with whom, how you feel when you do it, what you like about it, as well as what you don't like about it. Sound okay?

Client: Yeah, let's do it.

Therapist: Okay, Brian, let's summarize what we have discussed. You enjoyed hiking at the state park not too far away; you enjoyed going there with your wife; it was good exercise that invigorated you both, and it cleared your mind of stress. The one thing you think you might not like is that it may make you tired because you're out of shape. But you think this might improve as you got more hiking time in. Does that sound accurate?

Client: It does. I'm kinda looking forward to it. It would be nice to feel good again.

Therapist: Great. Now with all that in mind, can you commit to scheduling a time to go hiking and invite your wife to join you?

Client: I will. I'll ask my wife if she'll go with me on Saturday morning.

Therapist: Excellent.

Critique of the Community Reinforcement Approach Demonstration Vignette

The following points were made in the critique:

a. The focus of this session is on finding social activities that are rewarding and can replace alcohol-related activities that could trigger drinking.

b. Bowling is rejected due to strong association with drinking in the client's history.

c. Functional analysis is done to increase the probability that the client will engage in the desirable activity of hiking (treatment adherence); the client identifies the positive consequences of hiking and becomes more motivated to ask his wife to do this with him.

d. Asking the client to schedule the desirable activity is a means of "gentle accountability."

Additional point that could be made:

a. The therapist leads the client to the conclusion that bowling is not a desirable activity due to its potential trigger effect on drinking; better to take the time to lead the client to this conclusion than for the therapist to simply reject it himself.

b. Multiple therapeutic styles could be used to deliver this treatment, including the reflective-clarifying one seen here, to those more akin to a therapeutic coach or "cheerleader."

Comments you would like to make:

_____

_____

_____

_____

Homework: Communication skills are the focus of "Three Key Ingredients to Positive Social Interactions" and "What Comes After 'Hi'?" exercises in the *Group Therapy Homework Planner* (Bevilacqua). Another comprehensive exercise in socialization is "Communication Skills" (*Addiction Treatment Homework Planner* by Finley and Lenz). An excellent problem-solving homework assignment is "Problem-Solving: An Alternative to Impulsive Action" (*Adult Psychotherapy Homework Planner*, 2nd ed., by Jongsma). Another assignment from this same resource book is "Applying Problem-Solving to Interpersonal Conflict."

Assertiveness is addressed in the *Group Therapy Homework Planner* (Bevilacqua) through two exercises: "Is It Passive, Aggressive, or Assertive?" and "It's Okay to be Assertive." Life satisfaction is addressed in these exercises: "What Needs to be Changed in My Life?" and "What's Good About Me and My Life?" The exercise "Identify and Schedule Pleasant Activities" assists the client in exploring rewarding interests he might like to engage in (*Adult Psychotherapy Homework Planner*, 2nd ed., by Jongsma). Vocational dissatisfaction is the focus of these two homework assignments: "What Else Can I Do to Make Things Better?" and "How I Will Get What I Want" (*Group Therapy Homework Planner* by Bevilacqua) (see www.wiley.com/go/sudwb).

Community Reinforcement Approach Review

1. What are key characteristics of the community reinforcement approach?

Community Reinforcement Approach Review Test Question

1. In the community reinforcement approach, substance use behavior is replaced with which of the following?

    A. Addictive activities (e.g., computer games) that don't involve substance use
    B. Alternative, non-substance-using, and rewarding activities
    C. Alternative substance use that is nonaddicting
    D. Coping skills to manage the urges to use

Behavioral Couples Therapy

Our next set of objectives and treatment interventions is designed to capture the use of behavioral couples therapy. Goals of this therapy include reducing relationship conflict and increasing the nonusing partner's reinforcement of the client's sobriety. The therapist begins by developing with the couple a sobriety contract that stipulates abstinence, focuses couple interactions on present-day progress rather than reviewing hurts from the past, outlines the role of AA meetings, and schedules daily face-to-face talk time. Each partner is asked to make a list of pleasurable activities that can be processed and then scheduled into the daily routine of the couple. The couple is also taught communication and problem-solving skills. Role-plays are often used to facilitate implementation of these skills into the couple's everyday life. Finally, the recovery contract serves as a basis for reviewing the couple's progress and current relationship issues. Newly learned communication skills are strengthened with a focus on resolving issues respectfully.

Key Points

KEY CHARACTERISTICS OF BEHAVIORAL COUPLES THERAPY

- The purpose of behavioral couples therapy is to build support for abstinence and to improve relationship functioning.
- Arranges a daily "sobriety contract" in which the patient states his or her intent not to drink or use drugs, and the spouse expresses support for the patient's efforts to stay abstinent.
- Self-help meetings and drug urine screens are part of the contract for most patients. BCT also increases positive activities and teaches personal and interpersonal skills (e.g., communication, problem solving).

Table 5.5 contains examples of an objective and interventions reflective of behavioral couples therapy for SUD.

Table 5.5   Behavioral Couples Therapy Objectives and Interventions

Objective	Interventions
15. Participate in behavioral couples therapy designed to increase the non-substance-using partner's reinforcement of sobriety and to reduce relationship conflict.	1. Develop a sobriety contract with the couple that stipulates an agreement to remain abstinent, limits the focus of partner discussions to present-day issues rather than past hurtful behaviors, identifies the role of AA meetings, and schedules a daily time to share thoughts and feelings. 2. Ask each partner to make a list of pleasurable activities that could be engaged in together to increase positive feelings toward each other; process the list and assign implementation of one or more activities before the next session. 3. Teach the couple problem-solving skills (identify and pinpoint the problem, brainstorm possible solutions, list and evaluate the pros and cons of each solution, select and implement a solution, evaluate all parties' satisfaction with the action, adjust action if necessary); role-play the use of these skills applied to real-life issues of conflict for the couple. 4. In light of the recovery contract, review the client's sobriety experience and the couple's interaction since the last session; address any relationship conflicts, assisting the couple in improving their communication skills (e.g., "I" messages, reflective listening, eye contact, respectful responding) by using role-play in the session.

Demonstration Vignette
Behavioral Couples Therapy

Here we present the transcript of the dialogue depicted in the behavioral couples therapy vignette.

Therapist: Sarah, I want to welcome you to our counseling sessions. As you know, Brian and I have met a few times as he's begun his journey into abstinence from alcohol dependence. Some have said that recovery is a lifelong process, so he has just begun. Both of you have indicated a desire to work toward Brian's recovery. Just like drinking affects the marriage and the children, the spouse and the children have an impact on the alcohol user. In order to maximize the positive effect that a supportive partner can have, we'll be meeting in joint weekly sessions for the next five or six months. How does that sound?

Brian: I'm happy that Sarah is here today, and—

Therapist [interrupting Brian]: Brian, I think it may help the two of you communicate if you would look at Sarah and talk directly to her. Like this [looking at Sarah]: "Sarah, I'm glad you are here— [looking at Brian] and then go on to say what you were saying but say it to her.

Brian: Okay. Sarah, I'm glad you came today and that you're willing to help me. I do worry that you may never trust me again and you'll remind me of all my past failures and mistakes.

Sarah: Well, I can't say I'm 100 percent confident that you're going to stop drinking this time after all your broken promises to me, your mom, the kids, and even your boss. I'm shocked he hasn't fired you for all the days you've missed because of your drinking and being hungover.

Therapist: Sarah, your distrust is certainly warranted. Brian has earned that over the last eight years you've been together. But for Brian to succeed in this recovery attempt, he'll need your trust in small doses and over short periods of time until he earns more of it. And in this therapy, we'll need to keep the focus on the present and near future rather than bringing up the past. We'll talk frequently about where your trust level is, Sarah, as we move forward. It'll need to be based on the small successes we hope to have as recovery proceeds. Can you work with that?

Sarah: I'll try. There's just been so much hurt in the past, it'll be hard to leave it all behind.

Therapist: I understand that. Brian, do you understand Sarah's struggle? Tell her directly.

Brian: [looking at Sarah] I do understand, Sarah. I've put everyone through hell, and I want to change. I need your help.

Therapist: Part of this therapy involves making commitments and trying to stick to them. To help us with this, I'll be writing up a contract for us to review next time. One of the agreements in the contract will be this very issue—no talking about past behavior. The focus must be on present-day issues since recovery began. Other aspects in the contract are an agreement by Brian to remain abstinent, attend 90 AA meetings in 90 days, get a sponsor, and set aside 15 minutes each evening to talk to Sarah. In these talks he agrees to renew his pledge to be clean and sober for the next 24 hours. He'll also talk about any challenges he's having in remaining sober. Sarah must agree to listen without criticism or reminders of the past. She'll be as encouraging and supportive as she can be. What are your thoughts about the contract?

Sarah: I think it's a good idea. [To Brian] I know I'll have to watch myself. My first reaction is to be skeptical. [To therapist] We've been through a lot.

Therapist: You have been through a lot, Sarah. But your willingness to be here today tells me that you still have some hope for the future, and we'll try to build on that. Brian?

Brian: It's been hard for Sarah and me to talk about anything without arguing, so I'm worried about the agreement to talk every night for 15 minutes. But I want to try this time. If we have problems with it, should we bring it up here and try to work it out?

Therapist: Absolutely. You both have the same goal of a marriage and family free from alcohol. So if you can work together, it will improve your communication and make your relationship stronger. I'll have the contract ready for your review and signatures when we meet next week. Have a good week.

Critique of the Behavioral Couples Therapy Demonstration Vignette

The following points were made in the critique:

a. Risky abrupt intervention by the therapist to encourage direct communication of client with his wife; some clients will not respond well to such a confrontation.

b. Therapist is directing the wife's focus to present and future because it will be unproductive to spend time on actions in the past that have a negative association.

c. The contract is a written document that takes negotiation between parties; the goal is to facilitate positive behaviors that can be reinforced.

Additional points that could be made:

a. Instead of the therapist laying out the terms of the contract, time could be spent on the negotiation process, pulling both the husband and wife into listing elements that they would like to be included and the therapist functioning as a resource to clarify thoughts and feelings as well as suggesting other elements.

b. At the end, the therapist nicely highlights the hope for the future based on everyone's willingness to be engaged in the recovery process.

Comments you would like to make:

_____

_____

_____

_____

    Homework: A variation on the sobriety contract is a "Personal Recovery Plan" (*Addiction Treatment Homework Planner*, 4th ed., by Finley & Lenz), which identifies goals for recovery and then walks the client through several domains of life functioning, prompting them to identify supportive resources and relationships and ending with a commitment to a plan of action toward sobriety. Enjoyable activities are the focus of the exercise "Identify and Schedule Pleasant Activities," and resolving conflict is addressed in "Applying Problem-Solving to Interpersonal Conflict," as well as "How Can We Meet Each Other's Needs and Desires? and "Positive and Negative Contributions to the Relationship: Mine and Yours" (*Adult Psychotherapy Homework Planner*, 2nd ed., by Jongsma) (see www.wiley.com/go/sudwb).

Behavioral Couples Therapy Review

1. What are the key characteristics of behavioral couples therapy?

Behavioral Couples Therapy Review Test Question

1. Behavioral couples therapy emphasizes all of the following interventions *except* which of the following?

    A. Behavioral contracting
    B. Communication skills training
    C. Nondirective exploration of motivational ambivalence
    D. Positive reinforcement for sobriety-consistent behavior

Relapse Prevention Therapy

The last set of objectives and interventions reflects Relapse Prevention Therapy. Objectives 16 through 18 detail the client's action in implementing relapse prevention therapy strategies. The interventions for these objectives reflect the global and specific interventions that characterize this treatment. They include motivational interventions, teaching the distinction between a lapse and relapse, assessing risk factors, limiting exposure to triggers, teaching cognitive and behavioral coping skills, developing lifestyle balance by increasing rewarding activities that don't involve substance use, and encouraging the everyday implementation of skills learned in therapy.

Key Points

KEY CHARACTERISTICS OF RELAPSE PREVENTION THERAPY

- Motivational interventions
- Teaching the distinction between a lapse and relapse
- Assessing risk factors
- Limiting exposure to triggers
- Teaching cognitive and behavioral coping skills
- Developing lifestyle balance by increasing rewarding activities that don't involve substance use
- Encouraging the everyday implementation of skills learned in therapy

---

Table 5.6 contains examples of objectives and interventions reflective of relapse prevention therapy for SUD.

Table 5.6 Relapse Prevention Therapy Objectives and Interventions

Objectives	Interventions
16. Express a desire to maintain motivation for change as part of a relapse prevention strategy.	1. Explore motivation for change by looking at pros and cons, gradually moving the client toward committed action.
17. Verbalize an understanding of relapse prevention and the difference between a lapse and relapse.	1. Discuss with the client the distinction between a lapse and relapse, associating a lapse with an initial, temporary, and reversible use of a substance and relapse with the decision to return to a repeated pattern of abuse.
18. Identify potential situations that could trigger a lapse and implement strategies to manage these situations.	1. Evaluate past lapses and prescribe self-monitoring to assess current risk factors for lapses (or assign "Relapse Triggers" in the *Adult Psychotherapy Homework Planner*, 2nd ed., by Jongsma and/or the *Alcoholism and Drug Abuse Patient Workbook* by Perkinson).
	2. Use stimulus control techniques such as avoidance of specific triggers to reduce exposure to high-risk situations.
	3. Use instruction, modeling, imaginal rehearsal, role-play, and cognitive restructuring to teach the client cognitive-behavioral skills (e.g., relaxation, problem solving, social and communication skills, recognition and management of rationalization, denial, and apparently irrelevant decisions) for managing urges and other high-risk situations.
	4. Identify rewarding activities that do not involve substance use to balance the client's lifestyle.
	5. Instruct the client to routinely use strategies learned in therapy (e.g., problem solving, stimulus control, social skills, and assertiveness) while managing high-risk trigger situations (or assign "Aftercare Plan Components" in the *Adult Psychotherapy Homework Planner*, 2nd ed., by Jongsma).

Demonstration Vignette
Relapse Prevention Therapy

Here we present the transcript of the dialogue depicted in the Relapse Prevention Therapy vignette.

Therapist: How've you been doing this week, Brian?

Client: Not bad, really. I've stayed away from drinking again this week, and Sarah's been happy about that. I went to work every day and came straight home after instead of hanging out with the guys at the bar.

Therapist: Very good! Last week you mentioned that dealing with your co-workers, who were former drinking buddies, would be one of your high-risk situations for a relapse. How's that been going for you?

Client: I've really stayed away from that group, but I know Jack or Steve or one of the other guys is going to get in my face soon about going with them to the bar after work.

Therapist: I hear your concern about that pressure to join them, and that's a common issue that recovering people have to cope with. It's a very important first step that you've recognized this as a high-risk situation and you don't minimize the threat to your sobriety. This is a situation you're going to have to handle assertively, firmly, and politely. What do you think you should say when one of them asks you to meet them at the bar?

Client: [angrily] I've got to tell them to get out of my face! I can't do that anymore. They can go get sloshed, but leave me out of it.

Therapist: I hear you putting them off and turning them down, but perhaps you could be a little less aggressive but still be firm. You know what I mean?

Client: I just want them to get the message and leave me alone.

Therapist: I understand. But if you're hostile, they may get aggressive, and then the situation could escalate. How might you tell them in an assertive way that's not angry, that might not make them defensive?

Client: [thinking] Well, I don't know. I could just say I'm working on recovery and I can't be that close to alcohol.

Therapist: I think that's good. You might even thank them for asking, but tell them you can't be with them if alcohol is present. Remember, part of your recovery involves developing new friendships and new social activities that are not based on drinking.

Client: I guess that's better. It's not really their fault that I can't go with them.

Therapist: True. Now, like we've done before, let's try a rehearsal role-play. How about if I play Steve and you play yourself. Are you willing to try?

Client: All right.

Therapist: Hey, Brian, the guys are going to stop at the Bird's Nest after work and have a couple of beers. You want to come?

Client: Thanks for asking, Steve, but you know I'm trying this recovery thing, and I can't tip anything back right now.

Therapist: Yeah, I heard you were on the wagon. I've tried that too, but why don't you just come along and have a Coke or something? The guys would like to see you.

Client: I miss some of the old times too, but going to the bar with the booze flowing wouldn't be good for me. It's too risky. I've got to stay sober.

Therapist: Well, don't start thinking you're too good for us. You can cut down on your beers and still have a little fun with your buddies.

Client: Cutting back on my drinking isn't an option. I've tried that. This time I'm cutting it out completely and staying away from things that could get me to relapse. So thanks, but no thanks.

Therapist: That was excellent, Brian! You were direct and firm in your stand while not being aggressive. I like how you ignored Steve's thing about you being better than them. Ignoring is a good way to resist peer pressure without escalating the situation. How do you feel about this plan for coping with this high-risk situation?

Client: I like it better than getting in their face. I think I can do this.

Critique of the Relapse Prevention Therapy Demonstration Vignette

The following points were made in the critique:

a. The client identifies a high-risk situation for relapse: buddies at work inviting him to join them at their favorite bar; the client's coping skill thus far has been avoidance.

b. Therapist leads client to an assertive (not aggressive) response to address his former drinking buddies' request.

c. Role-play is used to build the assertive communication skill.

Additional points that could be made:

a. Therapist could have spent some time making the distinction between aggression and assertion and then exploring the advantages of assertiveness versus aggressiveness.

b. Role-play resulted in the client feeling more confident about implementing this new skill.

Comments you would like to make:

_____
_____
_____
_____

   Homework: In addition to the two assignments that are referenced in the Interventions in Table 5.6 ("Relapse Triggers" and "Aftercare Plan Components"), chemical dependence relapse prevention is also the focus of these four homework assignments: "Early Warning Signs of Relapse," "Identifying Relapse Triggers and Cues," "Relapse Prevention Planning," and "Relapse Symptom Line." Problem solving is addressed in "Applying Problem-Solving to Interpersonal Conflict." Finally, rewarding activities are the emphasis of "Identify and Schedule Pleasant Activities" (*Adult Psychotherapy Homework Planner*, 2nd ed., by Jongsma) (see www .wiley.com/go/sudwb).

Relapse Prevention Therapy Review

   1. What are key characteristics of Relapse Prevention Therapy?

Relapse Prevention Therapy Review Test Question

   1. Relapse prevention therapy emphasizes all of the following interventions *except* which of the following?

      A. Personal and interpersonal coping skills training
      B. Distinguishing between a lapse and relapse
      C. Exploring childhood antecedents to substance use
      D. Replacing substance use with other pleasurable activities

References

Bevilacqua, Louis. (2002). *Group Therapy Homework Planner*. New York: Wiley, 2002.

Finley, James R., & Brenda S. Lenz. (2003). *Addiction Treatment Homework Planner* (4th ed.). Hoboken, NJ: John Wiley.

Jongsma, Arthur E. (2006). *Adult Psychotherapy Homework Planner* (2nd ed.). Hoboken, NJ: Wiley.

Closing Remarks and Resources

As we note on the DVD, it is important to be aware that the research support for any particular EST supports the identified treatment as it was delivered in the studies supporting it. The use of only selected objectives or interventions from ESTs may not be empirically supported.

If you want to incorporate an EST into your treatment plan, it should reflect the major objectives and interventions of the approach. Note that in addition to their primary objectives and interventions, many ESTs have options within them that may or may not be used depending on the client's need (e.g., skills training). Most treatment manuals, books, and other training programs identify the primary objectives and interventions used in the EST.

An existing resource for integrating research-supported treatments into treatment planning is the Practice*Planners*® series[1] of treatment planners. The series contains several books that have integrated goals, objectives, and interventions consistent with those of identified ESTs into treatment plans for several applicable problems and disorders:

- ➢ *The Severe and Persistent Mental Illness Treatment Planner* (Berghuis, Jongsma, & Bruce)
- ➢ *The Family Therapy Treatment Planner* (Dattilio, Jongsma, & Davis)
- ➢ *The Complete Adult Psychotherapy Treatment Planner* (Jongsma, Peterson, & Bruce)
- ➢ *The Adolescent Psychotherapy Treatment Planner* (Jongsma, Peterson, McInnis, & Bruce)
- ➢ *The Child Psychotherapy Treatment Planner* (Jongsma, Peterson, McInnis, & Bruce)
- ➢ *The Veterans and Active Duty Military Psychotherapy Treatment Planner* (Moore & Jongsma)

---

[1] These books are updated frequently, check with the publisher for the latest editions and for further information about the Practice*Planners*®.

➤ *The Addiction Treatment Planner* (Perkinson, Jongsma, & Bruce)

➤ *The Couples Psychotherapy Treatment Planner* (O'Leary, Heyman, & Jongsma)

➤ *The Older Adult Psychotherapy Treatment Planner* (Frazer, Hinrichsen, & Jongsma)

Finally, it is important to remember that the purpose of this series is to demonstrate the process of evidence-based psychotherapy treatment planning for common mental health problems. It is designed to be informational in nature and does not intend to be a substitute for clinical training in the interventions discussed and demonstrated. In accordance with ethical guidelines, therapists should have competency in the services they deliver.

A

A Sample Evidence-Based Treatment Plan for Substance Use Disorders

Primary Problem: Alcohol Dependence

Behavioral Definitions:

1. Displays a maladaptive pattern of substance use, leading to clinically significant impairment or distress.
2. Demonstrates increased tolerance for the drug, as there is the need to use more to become intoxicated or a markedly diminished effect with continued use of the same amount of the substance.
3. Exhibits physical withdrawal symptoms (e.g., shaking, seizures, nausea, headaches, sweating) when going without the substance for any length of time, or a substance is taken to relieve or avoid withdrawal symptoms.
4. Fails to stop or cut down use of mood-altering drug once started, despite the verbalized desire to do so and the negative consequences continued use brings.
5. Demonstrates a great deal of time spent in activities necessary to obtain the substance, use the substance, or recover from its effects.
6. Reports suspension of important social or occupational role obligations because they interfere with using.

Diagnosis: Alcohol Dependence (303.90)

Long-Term Goals:

1. Accept the unmanageability over mood-altering substances, and participate in a recovery-based program.
2. Establish a sustained recovery, free from the use of all mood-altering substances.

Objectives	Interventions
1. Cooperate with medical assessment and an evaluation of the necessity for pharmacological intervention.	1. Refer the client to a medical health care provider to perform an assessment of possible medical effects of substance use, assess the need for psychotropic medication for any mental/emotional comorbidities, and discuss the use of acamprosate (Campral), naltrexone (Vivitrol), or disulfiram (Antabuse) where applicable.
2. Report acute withdrawal symptoms to the staff.	1. Assess and monitor the client's condition during withdrawal, using a standardized procedure (e.g., Narcotic Withdrawal Scale) as needed.

(continued)

Objectives	Interventions
3. Complete psychological testing or objective questionnaires for assessing substance dependence.	1. Administer to the client psychological instruments designed to objectively assess substance dependence (e.g., Substance Use Disorders Diagnostic Schedule-IV [SUDDS-IV], Substance Abuse Subtle Screen Inventory-3 [SASSI-3]); give the client feedback regarding the results of the assessment; readminister as needed to assess outcome.
4. Provide honest and complete information for a chemical dependence biopsychosocial history.	1. Complete a thorough family and personal biopsychosocial history that has a focus on addiction (e.g., family history of addiction and treatment, other substances used, progression of substance abuse, consequences of abuse).
5. Attend didactic sessions and read assigned material in order to increase knowledge of addiction and the process of recovery.	1. Assign the client to attend a chemical dependence didactic series to increase his/her knowledge of the patterns and effects of chemical dependence; ask him/her to identify several key points attained from each didactic and process these points with the therapist. 2. Assign the client to read a workbook describing evidence-based treatment approaches to addiction recovery (e.g., *Overcoming Your Alcohol or Drug Problem*, 2nd ed., by Daley and Marlatt); use the readings to reinforce key concepts and practices throughout therapy.
6. List and discuss negative consequences resulting from or exacerbated by substance dependence.	1. Ask the client to make a list of the ways chemical use has negatively impacted his/her life (or assign "Substance Abuse Negative Impact Versus Sobriety's Positive Impact" in the *Adult Psychotherapy Homework Planner*, 2nd ed., by Jongsma); process the list in individual or group sessions. 2. Use reflection to highlight the client's use of denial to minimize the severity of and negative consequences of substance abuse.
7. Explore and resolve ambivalence associated with commitment to change behaviors related to substance use and addiction.	1. Using a directive, client-centered, empathic style derived from motivational enhancement therapy (see *Motivational Interviewing* by Miller and Rollnick; and *Addiction and Change* by DiClemente), establish rapport with the client and listen reflectively, asking permission before providing information or advice. 2. Ask open-ended questions to explore the client's own motivations for change, affirming his/her change-related statements and efforts (see *Substance Abuse Treatment and the Stages of Change* by Connors, Donovan, and DiClemente). 3. Elicit recognition of the discrepancy gap between current behavior and desired life goals, reflecting resistance without direct confrontation or argumentation.
8. Commit self to an action plan directed toward termination of substance use.	1. Encourage and support the client's self-efficacy for change toward the goal of developing an action plan for termination of substance use to which the client is willing to commit.

Objectives	Interventions
9. Participate in behavioral couples therapy designed to increase the non-substance-using partner's reinforcement of sobriety and to reduce relationship conflict.	1. Develop a sobriety contract with the couple that stipulates an agreement to remain abstinent, limits the focus of partner discussions to present-day issues rather than past hurtful behaviors, identifies the role of AA meetings, and schedules a daily time to share thoughts and feelings.
	2. Ask each partner to make a list of pleasurable activities that could be engaged in together to increase positive feelings toward each other; process the list and assign implementation of one or more activities before the next session.
	3. Teach the couple problem-solving skills (identify and pinpoint the problem, brainstorm possible solutions, list and evaluate the pros and cons of each solution, select and implement a solution, evaluate all parties' satisfaction with the action, adjust action if necessary); role-play the use of these skills applied to real-life issues of conflict for the couple.
	4. In light of the recovery contract, review the client's sobriety experience and the couple's interaction since the last session; address any relationship conflicts, assisting the couple in improving their communication skills (e.g., "I" messages, reflective listening, eye contact, respectful responding) by using role-play in the session.
10. Verbalize an understanding of relapse prevention and the difference between a lapse and relapse.	1. Discuss with the client the distinction between a lapse and relapse, associating a lapse with an initial, temporary, and reversible use of a substance and relapse with the decision to return to a repeated pattern of abuse.
11. Identify potential situations that could trigger a lapse and implement strategies to manage these situations.	1. Evaluate past lapses and prescribe self-monitoring to assess current risk factors for lapses (or assign "Relapse Triggers" in the *Adult Psychotherapy Homework Planner*, 2nd ed., by Jongsma and/or the *Alcoholism and Drug Abuse Patient Workbook* by Perkinson).
	2. Use stimulus control techniques such as avoidance of specific triggers to reduce exposure to high-risk situations.
	3. Use instruction, modeling, imaginal rehearsal, role-play, and cognitive restructuring to teach the client cognitive-behavioral skills (e.g., relaxation, problem-solving, social and communication skills, recognition and management of rationalization, denial, and apparently irrelevant decisions) for managing urges and other high-risk situations.

B

Chapter Review Test Questions and Answers Explained

Chapter 1: What Are Substance Use Disorders?

1. After several months of substance use, Bill has begun using the substance when he awakens in the morning with some shakes and feelings of anxiety. He states that, "It calms me." Diagnostically, this pattern of use is considered a manifestation of which of the following:

   A. Anxiety
   B. Insomnia
   C. Tolerance
   D. Withdrawal

      A. *Incorrect*: Bill is trying to prevent withdrawal symptoms, one of which may be anxiety.
      B. *Incorrect*: Bill is trying to prevent withdrawal symptoms, one of which may be insomnia.
      C. *Incorrect*: Bill is trying to prevent withdrawal symptoms. It is likely that he has also developed a tolerance to the substance, which would be indicated by the presence of withdrawal symptoms upon removal of the substance, needing increased amounts of the substance to achieve intoxication or the desired effect, or by experiencing a markedly diminished effect with continued use of the same amount of the substance.
      D. *Correct*: This is considered a manifestation of withdrawal, which is indicated by use of the same substance (or another substance) or alcohol to relieve or avoid withdrawal symptoms.

2. True or False: According to the *DSM*, substance dependence is not diagnosed unless there is evidence of physiological tolerance or withdrawal.

False: Substance dependence can be diagnosed even though the patient shows no signs of physiological tolerance or withdrawal. The specifier "without physiological dependence" is used when the pattern of use meets the three-symptom criteria for dependence, but none of the symptoms are either physiological tolerance or withdrawal. This type of dependence would be characterized by the criteria reflecting a pattern of compulsive use of the substance (see criteria 3 through 7).

Chapter 2: What Are the Six Steps in Building a Treatment Plan?

1. Some patients with a substance use disorder demonstrate physiological tolerance; some do not. Some show problems in one area of functioning, whereas others may not. In which step of treatment planning would you record the particular expressions of substance use disorder for your individual client?

    A. Creating short-term objectives
    B. Describing the problem's manifestations
    C. Identifying the primary problem
    D. Selecting treatment interventions
        A. *Incorrect*: Expressions of the disorder, also referred to as manifestations, features, or symptoms, are described in Step 2 of treatment planning. They are not objectives for the client to achieve.
        B. *Correct*: Expressions of the disorder, also referred to as manifestations, features, or symptoms, are described in Step 2 of treatment planning.
        C. *Incorrect*: Expressions of the disorder, also referred to as manifestations, features, or symptoms, are described in Step 2 of treatment planning. They are expressions of the primary problem—the substance use disorder.
        D. *Incorrect*: Expressions of the disorder, also referred to as manifestations, features, or symptoms, are described in Step 2 of treatment planning. They are not interventions that the therapist will use to help the client achieve his or her objectives.

2. The statement "Learn and implement strategies for identifying, preventing, or coping with high-risk situations for relapse back into substance use" is an example of which of the following steps in psychotherapy treatment planning?

    A. A primary problem
    B. A short-term objective
    C. A symptom manifestation
    D. A treatment intervention

A. *Incorrect*: The primary problem (Step 1 in treatment planning) is the summary description, usually in diagnostic terms, of the client's primary problem.

B. *Correct*: This is a short-term objective (Step 5 in treatment planning). It describes a desired action of the client that is likely to help him or her reach a treatment goal.

C. *Incorrect*: Symptom manifestations (Step 2 in treatment planning) describe the client's particular expression (i.e., features or symptoms) of the primary problem.

D. *Incorrect*: A treatment intervention (Step 6 in treatment planning) describes the therapist's actions designed to help the client achieve his or her short-term objectives.

Chapter 3: What Is the Brief History of the EST Movement?

1. Which statement best describes the process used to identify ESTs?

   A. Consumers of mental health services nominated therapies.
   B. Experts came to a consensus based on their experiences with the treatments.
   C. Researchers submitted their works.
   D. Task groups reviewed the literature using clearly defined selection criteria for ESTs.

   A. *Incorrect*: Mental health professionals selected ESTs.
   B. *Incorrect*: Expert consensus was not the method used to identify ESTs.
   C. *Incorrect*: Empirical works in the existing literature were reviewed to identify ESTs.
   D. *Correct*: Review groups consisting of mental health professionals selected ESTs based on predetermined criteria such as *well-established* and *probably efficacious*.

2. Based on the differences in their criteria, in which of the following ways are *well-established* treatments different from those classified as *probably efficacious*?

   A. Only *probably efficacious* allowed the use of single-case design experiments.
   B. Only *well-established* allowed studies comparing the treatment to a psychological placebo.
   C. Only *well-established* required demonstration by at least two different, independent investigators or investigating teams.
   D. Only *well-established* allowed studies comparing the treatment to a pill placebo.

   A. *Incorrect*: Both sets of criteria allowed use of single-subject designs. *Well-established* required a larger series than did *probably efficacious* (see II under Well-Established and III under Probably Efficacious).

B. *Incorrect*: Studies using comparison to psychological placebos were acceptable in both sets of criteria (see IA under Well-Established and II under Probably Efficacious).

C. *Correct*: One of the primary differences between treatments classified as *well-established* and those classified as *probably efficacious* is that *well-established* therapies have had their efficacy demonstrated by at least two different, independent investigators (see V under Well-Established).

D. *Incorrect*: Studies using comparison to pill placebos were acceptable in both sets of criteria (see IA under Well-Established and II under Probably Efficacious).

Chapter 4: What Are the Identified Empirically Supported Treatments for Substance Use Disorders?

1. Which research-supported treatment for substance use disorders discussed in this chapter focuses primarily on helping individuals resolve their ambivalence about engaging in treatment and stopping substance use?

   A. Behavioral couples therapy
   B. Contingency management
   C. Motivational enhancement therapy
   D. 12-step facilitation

   A. *Incorrect*: Although motivation for change is a topic addressed in most therapies, it is the primary focus of motivational enhancement therapy.

   B. *Incorrect*: Although motivation for change is a topic addressed in most therapies, it is the primary focus of motivational enhancement therapy.

   C. *Correct*: As the name suggests, motivational enhancement therapy uses motivational interviewing techniques to help individuals resolve their ambivalence about engaging in treatment and stopping substance.

   D. *Incorrect*: Although motivation for change is a topic addressed in most therapies, it is the primary focus of motivational enhancement therapy.

2. In which research-supported treatment approach are patients given the chance to earn low-cost incentives in exchange for clean urine samples?

   A. Behavioral couples therapy
   B. Contingency management
   C. Motivational enhancement therapy
   D. 12-step facilitation therapy

   A. *Incorrect*: Although reinforcing positive change is part of most research-supported therapies, contingency management and some forms of community reinforcement use tangible, contingent rewards (e.g., prizes, goods, voucher for goods) to reinforce abstinence as evidenced by clean urine screens.

B. *Correct*: Contingency management and some forms of community reinforcement use tangible, contingent rewards (e.g., prizes, goods, voucher for goods) to reinforce abstinence as evidenced by clean urine screens.

C. *Incorrect*: Although reinforcing positive change is part of most research-supported therapies, contingency management and some forms of community reinforcement use tangible, contingent rewards (e.g., prizes, goods, voucher for goods) to reinforce abstinence as evidenced by clean urine screens.

D. *Incorrect*: Although reinforcing positive change is part of most research-supported therapies, contingency management and some forms of community reinforcement use tangible, contingent rewards (e.g., prizes, goods, voucher for goods) to reinforce abstinence as evidenced by clean urine screens.

Chapter 5: How Do You Integrate ESTs Into Treatment Planning?

Assessment/Psychoeducation

1. At what point in therapy is psychoeducation conducted?

    A. At the end of therapy
    B. During the assessment phase
    C. During the initial treatment session
    D. Throughout therapy

    A. *Incorrect*: Although some psychoeducation may be done at this phase of therapy, psychoeducation is conducted throughout therapy.
    B. *Incorrect*: Although some psychoeducation is commonly done at assessment, psychoeducation is conducted throughout therapy.
    C. *Incorrect*: Although psychoeducation is often done early in therapy, it continues throughout.
    D. *Correct*: Psychoeducation permeates all phases of therapy.

Motivational Enhancement Therapy

1. Although using techniques most associated with nondirective therapies, motivational enhancement therapy is guided by which of the following goals?

    A. To confront clients about the negative consequences of their substance use
    B. To help clients understand the developmental origins of their substance use
    C. To improve clients' understanding of the negative consequences of their substance use

D. To move clients through the stages of change toward action
  A. *Incorrect*: Although clients may take the therapeutic discussion in the direction of negative consequence of substance use, they are not confronted to consider them.
  B. *Incorrect*: Although clients may take the therapeutic discussion in the direction of development issues, increased understanding of them is not a primary goal of the therapy.
  C. *Incorrect*: Although a discussion of the negative consequences of substance use is a common topic brought up with clients, discussion of them is oriented toward increasing motivation to change.
  D. *Correct*: As the name suggests, motivational enhancement therapy uses motivational interviewing techniques to help clients resolve ambivalence about their motivation toward the goal of taking action to reduce or stop substance use.

Community Reinforcement Approach

1. In the community reinforcement approach, substance use behavior is replaced with which of the following?
  A. Addictive activities (e.g., computer games) that don't involve substance use
  B. Alternative, non-substance-using, and rewarding activities
  C. Alternative substance use that is nonaddicting
  D. Coping skills to manage the urges to use
    A. *Incorrect*: Alternative, non-substance-using, and rewarding activities are emphasized. There is no emphasis on how addicting they are.
    B. *Correct*: Alternative, non-substance-using, and rewarding activities are emphasized.
    C. *Incorrect*: Alternative, non-substance-using, and rewarding behavioral activities are emphasized.
    D. *Incorrect*: Although coping skills are taught in part to avoid or manage high-risk times, replacing substance use behavior with alternative, non-substance-using, and rewarding activities is emphasized.

Behavioral Couples Therapy

1. Behavioral couples therapy emphasizes all of the following interventions *except* which of the following?
  A. Behavioral contracting
  B. Communication skills training
  C. Nondirective exploration of motivational ambivalence
  D. Positive reinforcement for sobriety-consistent behavior

A. *Incorrect*: Behavioral contracting is a primary intervention in behavioral couples therapy.
B. *Incorrect*: Communication skills training is a primary intervention in behavioral couples therapy.
C. *Correct*: This intervention is more descriptive of motivational interviewing and motivational enhancement therapy.
D. *Incorrect*: Positive reinforcement, particularly by the partner of the client's positive behavior, is a primary intervention in behavioral couples therapy.

Relapse Prevention Therapy

1. Relapse prevention therapy emphasizes all of the following interventions *except* which of the following?

    A. Personal and interpersonal coping skills training
    B. Distinguishing between a lapse and relapse
    C. Exploring childhood antecedents to substance use
    D. Replacing substance use with other pleasurable activities

    A. *Incorrect*: Personal and interpersonal coping skills training is a primary intervention in relapse prevention therapy.
    B. *Incorrect*: Distinguishing between a lapse and relapse is a key concept in relapse prevention therapy.
    C. *Correct*: Although significant development issues would not be ignored in this therapy, it is more present-focused by design.
    D. *Incorrect*: Building a rewarding lifestyle, done in part by replacing substance use with other pleasurable activities, is a key emphasis of relapse prevention therapy.

STUDY PACKAGE
CONTINUING EDUCATION
CREDIT INFORMATION

Evidence-Based Treatment Planning for Substance Use Disorders

Our goal is to provide you with current, accurate and practical information from the most experienced and knowledgeable speakers and authors.

Listed below are the continuing education credit(s) currently available for this self-study package. *Please note: Your state licensing board dictates whether self study is an acceptable form of continuing education. Please refer to your state rules and regulations.*

Counselors: CMI Education Institute, Inc. is an approved provider of the National Board of Certified Counselors, NBCC Provider #: 5637. We adhere to NBCC Continuing Education Guidelines. This self-study package qualifies for **3.25** contact hours.

Social Workers: CMI Education Institute, Inc., #1062, is approved as a provider for social work continuing education by the Association of Social Work Boards (ASWB), 400 South Ridge Parkway, Suite B, Culpeper VA 22701. www.aswb.org. CMI Education Institute, Inc. maintains responsibility for the program. Licensed Social Workers should contact their regulatory board to determine course approval. Social Workers will receive **3.25** (clinical) continuing education clock hours for completing this self-study package. Course Level: All Levels.

Marriage and Family Therapists: This activity consists of **3.25** hours of continuing education instruction. Credit requirements and approvals vary per state board regulations. Please save the course outline, the certificate of completion you receive from this self-study activity and contact your state board or organization to determine specific filing requirements.

Psychologists: CMI Education Institute, Inc. is approved by the American Psychological Association to sponsor continuing education for psychologists. CMI maintains responsibility for this program and its content. CMI is offering these self-study materials for **3.0** hours of continuing education credit.

Addiction Counselors: CMI Education Institute, Inc. is an approved provider of continuing education by the National Association of Alcoholism & Drug Abuse Counselors (NAADAC), provider #: 00131. This self-study package qualifies for **4.0** contact hours.

Nurses/Nurse Practitioners/Clinical Nurse Specialists: This activity meets the criteria for an American Nurses Credentialing Center (ANCC) Activity CMI Education Institute, Inc. is an approved sponsor by the American Psychological Association, which is recognized by the ANCC for behavioral health related activities.

This self-study activity qualifies for **3.0** contact hours.

Other Professions: This activity qualifies for **3.25** clock hours of instructional content as required by many national, state and local licensing boards and professional organizations. Retain your certificate of completion and contact your board or organization for specific filing requirements.

Procedures:

1. Review the materials (publication and DVD).

2. If seeking credit, complete the posttest/evaluation form:

   -Complete posttest/evaluation in entirety; including your email address for the most prompt receipt of your certificate of completion.

   -Upon completion, mail to the address listed on the form along with the CE fee stated on the test. Tests will not be processed without the CE fee included.

   -Completed posttests must be received 6 months from the date of purchase.

Your completed posttest/evaluation will be graded. If you receive a passing score (70% and above), you will be emailed/faxed/mailed a certificate of successful completion with earned continuing education credits. (Please include your email address on the posttest/evaluation form for fastest response) If you do not pass the posttest, you will be sent a letter via email indicating areas of deficiency, and another posttest to complete. The posttest must be resubmitted and receive a passing grade before credit can be awarded. We will allow you to re-take as many times as necessary (with no additional fee) to receive a passing grade.

If you have any questions, please feel free to contact our customer service department at 1.800.844.8260.

CMI Education Institute
A Non-Profit Organization Connecting Knowledge with Need Since 1979

For additional forms and information on other Premier Education Solutions products, contact: **Customer Service; CMI Education;**
P.O. Box 1000; Eau Claire, WI 54702 (Toll Free, 7 a.m.-5 p.m. central time, 800-844-8260). www.cmieducation.org

CMI Education Institute
A Non-Profit Organization Connecting Knowledge with Need Since 1979

CMI EDUCATION INSTITUTE INC.   PREMIER PES   MEDS PDN

P.O. Box 1000
Eau Claire, WI 54702
(800) 844-8260

Evidence-Based Treatment Planning for Substance Use Disorders

Post Test/Evaluation Form

ZNT044620

Any persons interested in receiving credit may photocopy this form, complete and return with a payment of $15.00 per person CE fee. A certificate of successful completion will be sent to you.   To receive your certificate sooner than two weeks, rush processing is available for a fee of $10. Please attach check or include credit card information below.

Mail to: CMI Education, PO Box 1000, Eau Claire, WI 54702 or fax to: CMI Education (800) 554-9775 (fax both sides of page)

C.E. Fee: $15.00: (Rush Process Fee: $10) **Total to be charged:** _____

Credit card # _____   **Exp. Date:** _____

Signature: _____

V-Code* _____ (*MC/VISA/Discover: last 3-digit # on signature panel on back of card.) (*American Express: 4-digit # above account # on face of card.)

Name (please print): _____   _____   _____
                                                    LAST   FIRST   M.I.

Address: _____ Daytime Phone: _____

City: _____ State: _____ Zip: _____

Signature: _____ Email: _____ Fax: _____

• Date you completed the CMI Independent Package: _____

• Actual time (# of hours) taken to complete this offering: _____ hours

GENERAL COMMENTS

Please circle the number indicating your rating of each of the following items.

	Excellent				Poor
Relevance of objectives to overall goal	5	4	3	2	1
Effectiveness of the teaching/learning methods	5	4	3	2	1
Achievement of your personal objectives for completing this course	5	4	3	2	1
Similarity of program content to its description	5	4	3	2	1
Overall rating of package	5	4	3	2	1
How much did you learn as a result of this program? (5 being a great deal - 1 being very little)	5	4	3	2	1

PROGRAM OBJECTIVES

At the completion of this package, I have been able to achieve these seminar objectives:

Explain the process and criteria for diagnosing substance use disorders	Yes	No
List the six steps in building a clear psychotherapy treatment plan	Yes	No
Examine how empirically supported treatments for substance use disorders have been identified	Yes	No
Illustrate objectives and treatment interventions consistent with those of identified empirically supported treatments for substance use disorders	Yes	No
Describe how to construct a psychotherapy treatment plan and inform it with objectives and treatment interventions	Yes	No
identified empirically supported treatments for substance use disorders	Yes	No

PARTICIPANT PROFILE

1. Job Title _____   Employment Setting _____
2. Who paid the cost for this set?   Self _____   Employer _____
3. Do you utilize the internet? Yes _____ No _____   If so, where? Home _____ Work _____
4. What information did you hope to get from this audio/video/manual set? _____

Post Seminar Test Questions

1. According to the Diagnostic and Statistical Manual of Mental Disorders (DSM), substance dependence differs from substance abuse in which of the following ways?
A. Abuse requires at least three symptoms to be present within a 12-month period.
B. Abuse requires evidence of physiological tolerance or withdrawal, or compulsive use.
C. Dependence requires evidence of physiological tolerance or withdrawal, or compulsive use.
D. Dependence requires only one symptom to be present within a 12-month period.

2. According to the Diagnostic and Statistical Manual of Mental Disorders (DSM), there are two ways in which withdrawal could be evidenced in a patient's presentation: 1) withdrawal symptoms emerge within several hours to a few days after a reduction in heavy or prolonged alcohol or substance use, or 2) if the patient takes the same (or a closely related) substance to relieve or avoid withdrawal symptoms.
A. TRUE
B. FALSE

3. A patient's expression of substance dependence may involve tolerance or withdrawal. It may involve excessive time spent acquiring the substance or recovering from its effects. Different clients may show different features of dependence while still meeting its diagnostic criteria. In which of the following steps in the treatment planning process discussed in this program would a client's particular features of dependence be recorded?
A. Creating short-term objectives
B. Describing the problem's manifestations
C. Selecting therapeutic interventions
D. Specifying long-term goals

4. As discussed in this program, various reviewers have identified several interventions for substance use disorders that have empirical support for their efficacy. These include cognitive-behavioral treatments, community reinforcement, contingency management approaches, 12-step facilitation therapy, behavioral couples therapy, and motivational enhancement interventions. Which of the following of these approaches to treating substance use disorder emphasizes use of a "sobriety/abstinence contract?"
A. 12-Step facilitation therapy
B. Community reinforcement
C. Behavioral couples therapy
D. Motivational enhancement interventions

5. The concepts of acceptance (e.g., that addiction is a chronic progressive disease over which the sufferer has no control) and surrender (e.g., to a higher power and the fellowship of others) are central themes of which of the following research-supported treatment for substance-use disorders?
A. 12-Step facilitation therapy
B. Contingency management approaches
C. Behavioral couples therapy
D. Motivational enhancement interventions

6. Which of the following research-supported interventions for substance use disorders uses therapeutic techniques that derive historically from nondirective therapies, but are used to help the client move through stages of change toward action?
A. 12-Step facilitation therapy
B. Community reinforcement
C. Behavioral couples therapy
D. Motivational enhancement interventions

7. A common practice in relapse prevention therapy for substance use disorders is to help the client identify high-risk situations for a lapse and rehearse using skills learned in therapy to avoid or manage them.
A. TRUE
B. FALSE

8. Which of the following research-supported treatments for substance use disorders is characterized by the practice of giving patients low-cost incentives in exchange for drug-free urine samples.
A. 12-Step facilitation therapy
B. Contingency management approaches
C. Behavioral couples therapy
D. Motivational enhancement interventions

9. An emphasis in the community reinforcement approach to treating substance use disorders is to help the client develop new recreational activities and social networks intended to replace those associated with substance use.
A. TRUE
B. FALSE

10. Which of the following best describes the approach to creating an evidence-based treatment plan for eating disorders that is recommended in this program?
A. The therapist conducts cognitive behavioral therapy.
B. The therapist conducts behavioral couples therapy.
C. The therapist incorporates into therapy the objectives and interventions consistent with research-supported treatments.
D. The therapist incorporates into therapy the use of an objective measure of the eating disorder to track treatment progress.

11. In the Diagnostic and Statistical Manual of Mental Disorders (DSM), the terms substance dependence and substance abuse are applicable to which of the following?
A. Alcohol use only
B. All classes of substances
C. All non-alcohol related substances
D. All non-prescription substances

12. According to the Diagnostic and Statistical Manual of Mental Disorders (DSM), an individual can be correctly diagnosed as substance dependent even though there are no indicators of physiological dependence (i.e., tolerance or withdrawal).
A. TRUE
B. FALSE

13. A therapist decides to implement a system of rewards for negative urine screens with a client she is treating for alcohol dependence. In which of the following steps in the treatment planning process should this be recorded?
A. Creating short-term objectives
B. Describing the problem's manifestations
C. Selecting therapeutic interventions
D. Specifying long-term goals

14. A treatment plan contains the sentence, "Learn and implement skills designed to help prevent relapse of substance use." In which of the following steps in the treatment planning process would this be recorded?
A. Creating short-term objectives
B. Describing the problem's manifestations
C. Selecting therapeutic interventions
D. Specifying long-term goals

15. Which of the following research-supported treatments for substance use disorders is most likely to use a "sobriety contract" that therapy participants agree to and sign prior to beginning the therapy?
A. 12-Step facilitation therapy
B. Contingency management approaches
C. Behavioral couples therapy
D. Motivational enhancement interventions

16. According to reviewers cited in this program (i.e., Finney, Wilbourne, & Moos, 2007), which of the following is NOT a therapist- or therapeutic relationship-factor associated with better outcomes in the treatment of substance use disorders?
A. Confrontational
B. Empathic
C. Good alliance
D. Interpersonally skilled

17. The use of peer support, through encouragement of active participation in a specific type of peer group, is a central theme of which of the following research-supported treatments for substance use disorders?
A. 12-Step facilitation therapy
B. Cognitive behavioral therapy
C. Contingency management approaches
D. Motivational enhancement interventions

18. In the language of Relapse Prevention Therapy, there is commonly an emphasis made on the distinction between which of the following?
A. A lapse and a relapse
B. A relapse and recurrence
C. A slip and a setback
D. A trip and a fall

19. According to this program, the American Psychological Association defines an evidence-based practice as the integration of the best available research with clinical expertise in the context of patient characteristics, culture, and preferences.
A. TRUE
B. FALSE

20. In identifying the evidence-based treatments cited in this program, the authors (i.e., Jongsma & Bruce) have used which of the following methods?
A. Establishing their own specific criteria for research support and citing those treatments that meet them
B. Identifying patterns of agreement across reviewers, review groups, and evidence-based practice guideline developers
C. Identifying treatments most preferred by patients/client
D. Identifying treatments most preferred by therapists

For additional forms and information on other Premier Education Solutions products, contact: **Customer Service; CMI Education; P.O. Box 1000; Eau Claire, WI 54702 (Toll Free, 7 a.m.-5 p.m. central time, 800-844-8260). www.cmieducation.org**